quick crochet
huge hooks

SALLY HARDING

**photography by
John Heseltine**

C&T PUBLISHING

Quick Crochet Huge Hooks

First published in North America
by C&T Publishing Inc.,
PO Box 1456, Lafayette, CA 94549

Copyright © Octopus Publishing Group Ltd. 2005
Illustrations and Photographs © Octopus Publishing Group Ltd. 2005
Crochet designs and text copyright © Sally Harding 2005
10 9 8 7 6 5

ISBN 1-57120-312-5

A CIP record of this book is available from the British Library

Senior Executive Editor Anna Sanderson
Executive Art Editor Auberon Hedgecoe
Project manager Susan Berry
Design Anne Wilson
Illustrations Kate Simunek
Production Seyhan Esen

Set in Myriad

Color origination by Chroma Graphics, Singapore
Printed and bound in China by Toppan Printing Company Ltd.

quick crochet
huge hooks

contents

introduction...

In the middle of working on a book on giant-needle knitting, I couldn't resist the temptation to rush out and buy a huge crochet hook and see what kind of textures I could come up with. The results were even more exciting than I imagined they would be—really seductive fabrics with giant loops. And on top of this, I found it was amazingly quick, much faster than working with fat knitting needles. Since I am as passionate about crochet as I am about knitting—maybe even more so—producing a sister book on huge-hook crochet quickly became my next mission.

To entice absolute beginners into the craft and to provide inspiration for seasoned crocheters as well, I have filled the following pages with very simple projects made from a wide range of good-quality yarns, all worked on huge hooks. The inclusion of step-by-step instructions for all the basic crochet techniques means anyone can also use this book to learn crochet from scratch. Tips for adding fun trims—like pompoms, beads, fringe—are included, too.

My huge-hook crochet collection consists of scarves, bags, throws, a rug, and cushions. No complicated stitches have been used; in fact, the majority of projects are worked in simple single crochet—the easiest stitch to learn. Everything, with the exception of the String Shopper on page 54, is square, rectangular, or circular, so there's no complex shaping involved either.

Whenever I pick up a crochet hook and get going, I am reminded how enjoyable the actual process is, and working with great big hooks makes it even more so. To me, the versatility of crochet textures surpasses that of knitting—you can make just about any type of textile with crochet techniques, from fine intricate laces to draping wool scarves and sweaters or stiff string baskets. And it's so easy! Only one loop on the hook at a time also makes it hassle-free to stop and start, or to carry around wherever you go.

To give you a taster for the variety of crochet textures, I've included a range of yarn types—fine ones, superfat ones, rag strips, and string. Because the patterns are so easy—especially the scarves—I hope you'll use them as starters for your own original creations worked in any yarn you fancy. The beauty of huge-hook crochet is that the big loops show off the seductiveness of whatever threads you use and it's all finished in a flash. A scarf can be ready to wear in a few hours or a throw in a couple of days.

Like most crochet enthusiasts, I love introducing newcomers to this enjoyable craft and encouraging lapsed crocheters to look around and see all the exciting new yarns they can try. Huge-hook crochet will surely capture your imagination once you get started.

—**Sally Harding**

huge-hook know-how

crochet basics...

There's no better way to learn to crochet than with a huge hook. The big loops are easy to see and quick to make. As a recent convert to huge-hook crochet, I would now always advise learners to avoid starting out with fine hooks—they make the craft look difficult to master, which it definitely is not. Begin with big, bold, beautiful loops and once you can crochet with ease, fine laces will be as easy as pie.

This chapter includes everything an absolute beginner needs to know to learn to crochet, from forming the first loop to working the tallest basic stitches. Crocheters who haven't crocheted for a number of years can use the instructions as a refresher course and for the huge-hook tips.

Before you get crocheting, read this page and the next and have a look at pages 12–15. They provide an introduction to yarns for huge hooks, explain what "huge" hooks are, and illustrate the scope and versatility of the resulting stunning textures.

yarns for huge hooks

The first sight of huge hooks usually makes one think of giant yarns and thick, unyielding textures. This couldn't be farther from the truth. Superthick yarns can be worked with huge hooks, but so can fine and medium-weight yarns and strings and twines. How dense and stiff, or airy and flexible, the crochet fabric is depends on how thick the yarn is, how many strands are used together, and how huge the hook is. Any yarn can be used for huge-hook crochet. You can use it on its own as a single strand, or use several strands at once to thicken it, or twist it around other yarns to make your own version.

Crochet fabrics can also be formed with fabric strips. "Rag" crochet is ideal for bags and rugs, and I can't praise it enough. Making your own yarn from fabric remnants or old clothes opens up an exciting world of color and texture.

To see just a few of the possibilities for unique huge-hook textures, turn to pages 12–15 for some life-size samples.

choosing huge hooks

My choice of what constitutes a "huge" hook is purely arbitrary. The range starts with a 10.00mm (US size N-13) hook and ends with a 20.00mm (US size S)—the hugest one I've been able to find. I decided to start the range with a 10.00mm (US size N-13) hook because until fairly recently it was the largest around and, though always intrigued by it, I was never quite sure what anyone did with it—at a time when superfat yarns were a rarity. Placed next to a standard-size hook, a 10.00mm (US size N-13) hook still looks truly huge.

Most of the designs in this book are worked with 12.00mm (US size O/P-15) and 15.00mm (US size Q) hooks, but lots are worked with a 10.00mm (US size N-13)—so you can start with these if you find holding a bigger hook awkward at first. Two designs, the Pompom Scarves on pages 50–53, are worked with the supergiant 20.00mm (US size S). If you decide you love using this giant, I leave it to you to try making scarves galore, or even throws, with it.

To find huge hooks, look in local stores or surf the net—see page 126 for my favorite sites. For a guide to comparative hook sizes, see page 127.

20.00mm (US size S)

15.00mm (US size Q)

12.00mm (US size O/P-15)

10.00mm (US size N-13)

huge-hook textures

The life-size crochet texture samples on these two pages and the two that follow show just a few of the many yarns you can use with huge hooks. All the swatches are worked in simple single crochet, each with a different hook size.

Included in the yarns are mohair, cotton, tape, superthick wool, chunky chenille, and fabric strips.

Crochet lends itself to anything malleable and other textures you could try out are leather, raffia, string, and wire.

Airy crochet textures are perfect for scarves and lightweight throws; medium-density ones make good cushion covers, warm throws, and floppy bags; while really dense crochet is ideal for stand-alone bags, baskets, and rugs.

Single crochet worked with a 10.00mm (US size N-13) crochet hook, a medium-weight cotton yarn, and a medium-weight mohair yarn.

Single crochet worked with a 12.00mm (US size O/P-15) crochet hook, cotton tape yarn, a chunky chenille yarn, and narrow silk fabric strips.

Single crochet worked with a 20.00mm (US size S) crochet hook, a superthick wool yarn, and a novelty tape yarn (see page 126 for where to obtain this unusual yarn).

Single crochet worked with a 15.00mm (US size Q) crochet hook and wide silk fabric strips.

learning to crochet...

The best way to pick up crochet techniques is to have someone sitting by your side showing you how it's done. But if you're not lucky enough to have a personal tutor, here are clear, simple instructions for teaching yourself the main crochet stitches.

If you're starting to learn crochet from scratch, purchase a 12.00mm (US size O/P-15) hook and some chunky wool or synthetic wool-type yarn. Wool yarns are easy to manipulate because they have just the right amount of elasticity to glide on and off the hook with ease. A 12.00mm (US size O/P-15) hook is nice and big but more manageable for a beginner than the two largest sizes.

All crochet starts with a simple sliding knot called a "slip knot." Before making this first loop, try various ways of holding your hook and yarn to familiarize yourself with these simple tools of the craft.

holding the yarn

In crochet, the yarn is held in the left hand and the hook in the right (left-handers will have to reverse everything, using a mirror for the illustrations). There are any number of ways to lace the yarn around the fingers of the left hand and the lacing shown here (see right) is a popular method. Try this lacing, then gently pull the tail end of the yarn. The aim is for the fingers to hold the yarn with a bit of tension, allowing it to slide freely over the tip of the index finger as more yarn is needed to create the stitches. If you first learned to crochet with a different lacing technique, stick to it, because you will probably have better control with the method you learned first. For instance, many crocheters feed the yarn over the tip of the middle finger rather than the index finger, grasping the crochet between the index finger and thumb rather than between the middle finger and thumb.

holding the hook

The knife position (see below) is probably the best way to hold a huge hook if you are an absolute beginner, because it puts less pressure on the wrist. But try the "pencil" position, too, when learning how to make chain stitches (see page 18) just in case it suits you better.

TENSIONING YARN

KNIFE POSITION

PENCIL POSITION

making the first loop

1 Position the yarn and hook as explained on the previous page, then pinch the tail end of the yarn between the thumb and middle finger of the left hand. Grab the yarn with the hook and twirl the tip around the yarn in the direction shown by the arrow to form a loop on the hook.

2 To prevent the new loop on the hook from closing up too tightly, grip the bottom of it and the tail end of the yarn between the left thumb and middle finger. Move the hook around the yarn as shown by the arrow to form a "wrap" around the hook.

3 Now draw the "wrap" on the hook through the loop as shown by the arrow (A). This creates a slip knot on the hook (B). Pull both ends of the yarn to tighten the knot under the hook, but keep it loose enough to allow the loop to expand freely.

basic stitch symbols

Crochet patterns are often given in symbols. Even if you are an absolute beginner, it's a good idea to learn the symbols for the main crochet stitches right away. They show clearly how the stitches relate to each other sizewise and how they fit together in rows (see page 21). The crochet symbols here are a commonly used set. Different countries use slightly different symbols—all are easy to learn and bear a resemblance to the stitches they represent.

⊙ = first foundation
◯ = chain (ch)
⌒ = slip stitch (sl st)
+ = single crochet (sc)
T = half double crochet (hdc)

Ŧ = double crochet (dc)
Ⅎ = treble (tr)

preparing the foundation...

To start a piece of crochet, you create a base on which to work the first row of stitches. For a simple rectangular piece of crochet, this base consists of a length of chain stitches called a "foundation chain."

Easy crochet stitches to learn, chain stitches are also used at the beginning of rows as part of the selvage and in combination with other stitches to form all kinds of crochet textures and laces.

If you are a novice, before trying to make your first chain stitches, practice making slip knots (see page 17) until you can make one without looking at the illustrations. Mastering your first loop will teach you good yarn and hook control and give you the confidence to proceed, so don't rush it. Each repetition will improve your dexterity.

making a foundation chain

Crochet instructions start by telling you how many chains to make as the foundation for your first row of stitches. If 30 foundation chains are required, the instructions say "ch30." Making a chain stitch is as easy as it looks, but it takes a little practice until you can make them with just the right degree of tightness. Beginners should err on the side of loops that are a bit too loose, rather than too tight. With a little practice your fingers will find the right movements to make perfectly formed, even chains.

1 Make a slip knot, then grab the yarn with the hook as shown by the arrow (at the same time you can swivel the left hand slightly so you are wrapping the yarn with the left hand and grabbing with the hook simultaneously to speed up the movement).

2 Holding the slip knot between the middle finger and the thumb of the left hand, pull the yarn wrapped around the hook through the loop on the

hook to complete your first chain stitch. These first two steps are called in crochet terminology "yo (yarn over hook) and draw a lp (loop) through."

3 Make as many chains as required. Always count the stitches in your completed foundation chain to double check, but don't count the loop on the hook.

learning single crochet...

The first crochet stitch a beginner should learn is single crochet. It can be worked in combination with other crochet stitches to form texture patterns or on its own to create a crochet textile called "single crochet." Because of its ease of execution, single crochet has been used for many of the projects in this book. Beginners will love how easy it is to master.

The most versatile of all crochet stitches, single crochet can be worked tightly for firm textiles or loosely for airy ones. All the swatches on pages 12–15 have been worked back and forth in rows of single crochet. A smoother surface is achieved when the stitches are worked in the round, as on the bags on pages 60–67.

working single crochet

The steps on this page explain how to make single crochet stitches on a foundation chain. All individual single crochet stitches are made in the same way—the only variation is what you work them into. The first row is worked into a chain and the following rows are worked into the stitches of the previous row. Practice working single crochet into a chain as here until you get the hang of it, then turn to page 22 for how to work the following rows.

1 Make a foundation chain of about 12 chains. Holding the chains with the left hand, insert the hook from front to back through the *second* chain from the hook, wrap the yarn over the hook as shown by the arrow, and draw a loop of the yarn through the chain—there are now two loops on the hook. (You can insert the hook under one or two strands of the chain, but inserting it under one, as here, is easier for a beginner—see page 31 for a variation.)

2 Next, wrap the yarn over the hook ("yarn over" or "yo") and draw it through the two loops on the hook. This completes the first single crochet—called "sc." In a crochet pattern, what you have just done is called "1sc in 2nd ch from hook."

3 Work one single crochet in each of the remaining chains in the same way to complete the first row.

learning double crochet...

After single crochet, the two most frequently used crochet stitches are half double crochet and double crochet. Like single crochet stitches, each of these can be used in combination with other stitches for a variety of crochet textures or on their own. Half doubles are slightly taller than single crochet and doubles are slightly taller than half doubles (see symbols on pages 17 and 22). Double crochet stitches used on their own create a more airy, less firm textile than single crochet or half double crochet, which makes it more pliable and softer.

Try both these stitches with the same yarn and hook that you used to make a swatch of single crochet to see how the stitches compare.

working half doubles

Make sure you have completely mastered single crochet before trying half doubles. The method of working is similar, so if you can work single crochet effortlessly, learning half doubles will be a cinch. Follow these steps to work your first row, then turn to page 22 to learn how to work the following rows.

1 Make a foundation chain of about 13 chains. Wrap the yarn over the hook ("yarn over" or "yo"), simultaneously grabbing the yarn with the hook and moving the yarn forward slightly with the left hand to facilitate the movement. Then with the "wrap" in place, insert the hook from front to back through the *third* chain from the hook (under one or two strands of the chain), work a "yarn over" as shown by the arrow, and draw a loop through the chain—there are now three loops on the hook.

2 Next, work a "yarn over" and draw it through all three loops on the hook as shown by the arrow. This completes the first half double—called "hdc."

In a crochet pattern, what you have just done is called "1hdc in 3rd ch from hook."

3 Work one half double in each of the remaining chains in the same way to complete the first row of half double crochet.

HALF DOUBLE CROCHET

1

2

3

working doubles

Follow the steps on this page to work the first row of the simple double crochet textile. Then turn to page 22 to learn how to work more rows.

Practice making doubles before you try making the taller crochet stitches explained on page 23. The technique for making these taller stitches—called trebles, double trebles, triple trebles, and quadruple trebles—is almost exactly the same, except that they are started with more wraps on the hook.

1 Make a foundation chain of about 14 chains. Wrap the yarn over the hook ("yarn over" or "yo"). Then insert the hook from front to back through the *fourth* chain from the hook, work a "yarn over" as shown by the arrow, and draw a loop through the chain—there are now three loops on the hook.

2 Next, work a "yarn over" and draw it through the first two loops on the hook as shown by the arrow— two loops now remain on the hook.

3 Work a "yarn over" and draw it through the two loops on the hook as shown by the arrow. This completes the first double—called "dc." In a crochet pattern, what you have just done is called "1dc in 4th ch from hook."

4 Work one double in each of the remaining chains in the same way to complete the first row of double crochet.

DOUBLE CROCHET

1

2

3

4

how to turn for next row...

rows in symbols

This is where crochet symbols prove their worth. A few rows of singles, half doubles, and doubles shown in symbols give an understanding at a glance of how many chain stitches you'll need at the beginning of a row (called "turning chain"). They also show how the three chains at the beginning of a row of double crochet are a substitute for the first double (and are counted as "one" stitch). See page 17 for the symbol key.

SINGLE CROCHET

HALF DOUBLE CROCHET

DOUBLE CROCHET

The first row of a rectangular piece of crochet is worked into a length of chain stitches as explained on pages 18 through 21. On the following rows the stitches are worked into the stitches of the previous row.

After completing the first row, turn the crochet so the other side of the stitches are facing you and the hook and the loop on it are at the right-hand edge. Crochet instructions will always remind you at the end of a row to "turn" the work. In order to bring the yarn up to the height of the stitch you are working, you work one or more chain stitches at the edge of the crochet before working into the top of the row below. If working single crochet, make one chain; for half double crochet, work two chains; and for double crochet, work three chains (see below).

To complete the second row of single crochet or of half double crochet, work one stitch into each stitch in the row below, inserting the hook under both strands of the chain-shaped loop at the top of the stitch (see arrow). To complete the second row of double crochet, skip the first stitch below and work one stitch into the top of the second stitch (see arrow), then work one stitch into each of the remaining stitches. Work the last double crochet in the third of the three chains at the edge (see symbols left). Work all the following rows in the same way.

SINGLE CROCHET

HALF DOUBLE CROCHET

DOUBLE CROCHET

more stitches...

There are only two more basic stitches to learn in order to follow any possible crochet pattern—slip stitches and trebles. A slip stitch is the shortest crochet stitch, and a treble is the first of a series of the tallest crochet stitches.

working slip stitches

Rows of slip stitches are rarely used to form a crochet fabric, but a single row of slip stitches in a contrasting color can be used to create a neat, simple edging (see V-stitch Bag on page 67). More commonly, a single slip stitch is used as a connecting stitch to join a foundation chain into a ring or to join the yarn to a new position on the crochet fabric.

Slip stitches along a row

To work slip stitches along a row (see top right), insert the hook into the next stitch and wrap the yarn over the hook as shown by the arrow, then draw the yarn through the stitch and the loop on the hook in one movement—called "1 sl st."

Joining with a slip stitch

Individual slip stitches are used in many patterns in this book to join a foundation ring, the base for a piece of circular crochet. First make as many chain stitches as instructed, then insert the hook through the first chain and draw a loop through the chain and the loop on the hook (see center right). This is called "join with a sl st in first ch to form a ring."

working taller stitches

Simple trebles are worked in almost exactly the same way as doubles except that each stitch is started with two wraps on the hook instead of one and the hook is inserted into the *fifth* chain from the hook in the foundation chain. All the loops are then

SLIP STITCHES ALONG A ROW

JOINING WITH A SLIP STITCH

WORKING A TREBLE

worked off two at a time, as for doubles. The second and following rows of trebles are worked as for doubles, except four chains (instead of three) are worked at the start of the row for "turning" chains.

Taller trebles—double trebles, triple trebles, and quadruple trebles—are begun with three, four, or five wraps on the hook, and are worked using the same principle as trebles. Your pattern will state how many "turning" chains to use for these stitches.

increasing and decreasing...

Adding more stitches to a row of crochet is a technique called "increasing." Reducing the number of stitches is called "decreasing." Adding stitches on a piece of straight crochet widens the fabric and subtracting stitches narrows it, so these simple techniques are used for shaping your crochet.

Adding stitches in crochet is much simpler than in knitting, because it is so easy to work two or more stitches into the same spot. Subtracting from the number of stitches is just as easy—you can either skip stitches in the row below or half-finish two or more stitches (leaving the last loop of each stitch on the hook) and then join them by drawing a single loop through all the stitches. Your crochet pattern will tell you exactly how to work increases and decreases, but have a look at these very simple ones to understand the principle of the techniques.

working a simple increase

To add one stitch in a row of single crochet, just work two single crochet into the same stitch in the row below (see below left). This is called "2sc in next sc."

working a simple decrease

To decrease one stitch in a row of single crochet, draw a loop through each of the next two stitches, then draw a loop through all three loops on the hook as shown by the arrow (see bottom left). In a crochet pattern this is called "[insert hook in next sc, yo and draw a lp through] twice, yo and draw through all 3 lps on hook."

SIMPLE INCREASE

SIMPLE DECREASE

fastening off

When your piece of crochet is finished there will still be one loop on the hook. Securing this last loop so that your crochet does not unravel is called "fastening off." To fasten off, first cut the yarn—called "break off"— leaving a tail of yarn at least 6in/15cm long. Then draw the yarn end through the loop, and pull tight (see below).

following a crochet pattern...

The step-by-step instructions on the previous pages are a sound preparation for following any crochet pattern. They include an introduction to crochet terminology and abbreviations and how to work all the basic stitches found in crochet patterns. Special stitch patterns that are a combination of or a manipulation of basic stitches are always explained fully within a pattern.

Crochet patterns are generally all laid out in a similar way. They start by giving the size of the finished item. Following this is a list of yarn, hooks, and any other materials you'll need. Next comes the recommended gauge (see right) and any special tips you need to read before starting.

crochet abbreviations

Abbreviations in the row-by-row instructions of a crochet pattern make the patterns shorter, and easier and quicker to follow. Crochet terminology and abbreviations may seem confusing at first glance, but you will quickly realize that they make the patterns crystal clear; they are logical and really easy to learn. For example, "1sc in next st" means work one single crochet stitch in the next stitch in the row below. For easy reference, all the crochet abbreviations used in this book are given at the back (see page 127).

tip boxes in the patterns

Tip boxes and special how-to boxes are sprinkled throughout the instructions for the huge-hook designs. Pay special attention to these and to the Before You Start sections at the beginning of the patterns—they are the tips an advanced crocheter would give you if they were letting you in on their years of experience.

gauge

Everybody crochets with their own personal style. Several crocheters sitting side by side using the same size hook and yarn and working the same number of stitches will create pieces of crochet of a similar size but not precisely the same. Because there is no right or wrong crochet tightness, there's no need to try to alter your own style. Every crochet pattern specifies what size of stitch you should aim to achieve—this is called the "gauge." A gauge tells you how many stitches and rows there should be over 4in (10cm) of crochet. Before you begin a crochet pattern you can test your gauge by making a swatch of crochet and measuring the number of stitches and rows to 4in (10cm). If necessary, you can use a different hook size to increase or decrease the size of the stitches. However, if you are a beginner working with huge hooks, don't be too concerned about stitch size. Gauge will become more important when you start crocheting fitted garments, but for now just have fun with huge loops. If in doubt, err on the side of forming slightly looser loops so your huge hook can glide easily in and out of the stitches.

25

projects

Warm and cozy, this narrow wool scarf is the quickest project in the book to work. It is crocheted with a huge hook that is 15 millimeters in diameter (US size Q)—the second largest hook on the market. Worked end to end, instead of side to side in the usual way, it is 62 stitches long

three-row scarf

but only three rows wide! Because it is made entirely in double crochet, it is perfect for a beginner who wants to practice crocheting these simple, tall stitches. After speeding through the scarf, take your time to weave in and knot on the elegant fringe, using a superchunky variegated wool yarn in your chosen color.

here's how...

The foundation-chain edge of this scarf looks better if each stitch in the first row is worked into the back loop of each chain. This makes the first row of this scarf slower, but the last two go quickly.

how big is it?
The finished scarf measures approximately 3³/₄in/9cm wide (width of center section, not flared ends) x 54¹/₄in/140cm long, excluding fringe.

which stitches?
Double crochet (dc)

how much yarn?
MC = superchunky wool yarn in main color
    1 x 3¹/₂oz/100g ball Rowan *Big Wool*
    (lime—shade no. 029—or chosen color)
CC = superchunky variegated wool yarn in contrasting color
    small amount of Rowan *Biggy Print*
    (variegated mauve and cherry—shade no.
    246—or chosen color)
(*See page 124 for yarn tips*)

which hooks?
15.00mm and 20.00mm (US sizes Q and S) crochet hooks

or make this!
With one ball of Rowan *Big Wool* for the main color you can make a longer scarf—65in/169cm long—if you like. Just make 77 chains to start, for a scarf with 75 stitches.

what gauge?
4 sts and 3 rows to 3¹/₂in/9cm measured over dc using MC and 15.00mm (US size Q) hook.

before you start
- There is no need to check your gauge before beginning, as an exact scarf size is not essential.
- If you don't have a 20.00mm (US size S) crochet hook for working the foundation chain, use the 15.00mm (US size Q) and work very loosely.
- *For crochet abbreviations, turn to page 127.*

make the foundation chain
The scarf is worked from end to end instead of from side to side in the usual way.
Using a 20.00mm (US size S) hook and MC, ch64. Change to 15.00mm (US size Q) hook.
1st row 1dc in 4th ch from hook, 1dc in each of rem 60ch. Turn.
2nd row Ch3 (to count as first dc), skip first dc and work 1dc in next dc, 1dc in each of rem dc, ending with 1dc in 3rd of ch3. Turn. (62 sts)
3rd row As for 2nd row.
Fasten off by cutting yarn, passing yarn end through loop on hook, and pulling tight.

finishing touches
Before beginning fringe, weave in any loose ends.
Fringe
For each end of scarf make fringe as foll:
Cut five strands of CC each 37¹/₂in/95cm long.
Using your fingers, weave one strand of CC in and out of first 6 sts of first row of dc; then weave same strand back through same sts but *over* sts the first weaving went *under* and *under* sts the first weaving went *over*. Adjust these two fringe strands so they are equal lengths. Weave strands through other two

rows in same way. Weave rem two strands through gaps at tops of first 8 sts of first and second rows (at base of sts of row above). Knot tog two ends of each woven strand close to edge of scarf to secure. Then knot each length of fringe at end (about 7$\frac{1}{2}$in/19cm from edge of scarf) and trim off yarn $\frac{1}{4}$in/6mm from knot.

make a chain edge like this!

For a professional finish, you can make the foundation-chain edge of your crochet match the edge along the final row of crochet. To do this, work each stitch in the first row of stitches into the back loop of each chain as shown by the arrow above. This leaves a neat edge of linked chain stitches along the edge that exactly matches the linked chain along the top of the final row of crochet stitches. It can be hard to identify the back loop of the foundation chain on big loops, so you might want to practice this first with a 10.00mm (US size N-13) hook before starting your scarf.

alternative scarf

For an alternative, work the scarf with only two rows, then work single crochet in a contrasting color evenly around the edge, with three stitches in each corner.

striped mohair scarf

The lofty, airy lightness of this narrow scarf (left) is achieved quite simply—by working medium-weight and lightweight yarns with a huge hook. Though the predominant feel of the scarf is of a soft mohair, it also contains the contrasting textures of chunky chenille and a cotton and silk blend yarn. A linen tape yarn, woven along the length of the stitches as a finishing touch, sparks off these subtle stripes. Because each row of the scarf is worked end to end instead of from side to side in the usual way, the yarn ends form a self-fringe. Instructions for working a wider version of the scarf (see right) are given in the tip box on page 35.

here's how...

The instructions here are for the narrow scarf on page 32. If you want to make the wider scarf on page 33, see the tip box opposite.

how big is it?
The finished scarf measures approximately 3³/₄in/9.5cm wide x 52in/130cm long, excluding fringe.

which stitches?
Single crochet (sc)

how much yarn?
A = chunky chenille yarn in first color
  1 x 3¹/₂oz/100g ball Rowan *Chunky Cotton Chenille* in chosen color (aqua blue—shade no. 392—or chosen color)
B = medium-weight mohair yarn in second color
  1 x 1³/₄oz/50g ball Rowan *Kid Classic*

(light blue—shade no. 818—or chosen color)
C = fine mohair yarn in third color
  1 x 1oz/25g ball Rowan *Kid Silk Haze*
  (grape—shade no. 600—or chosen color)
D = lightweight silk and cotton yarn in fourth color
  1 x 1³/₄oz/50g hank Rowan *Summer Tweed*
  (orange—shade no. 509—or chosen color)
E = viscose and linen tape yarn in fifth color
  1 x 1³/₄oz/50g ball Rowan *Linen Print*
  (variegated pastels—shade no. 345—or chosen color)
(*See page 124 for yarn tips*)

which hook?
10.00mm (US size N-13) crochet hook

what gauge?
8 sts and 11¹/₂ rows to 4in/10cm measured over sc stripe patt using 10.00mm (US size N-13) hook.

alternative colorways
You can use yarns left over from this project or others in the book to make more scarves in your own stripe sequences. The trick to a successful design is to keep your palette limited and to use a mixture of yarn textures as shown here. Before starting your scarf, crochet small striped swatches to try out your color combinations and stripe widths.

before you start

- There is no need to check your gauge before beginning, as an exact scarf size is not essential.
- To create a neat chain edge along the foundation-chain edge of the scarf, see page 31.
- Remember to work each row of the scarf with a new length of yarn, leaving a long loose end at the beginning and end of each row. These ends form the "self-fringe." Leave ends at least 6in/15cm long. If making the wider version (see right), leave 8in/20cm ends.
- *For crochet abbreviations, turn to page 127.*

make the foundation chain

The scarf is worked from end to end instead of from side to side in the usual way.

Using a 10.00mm (US size N-13) hook and one strand A and leaving a long loose end before first chain, ch104 loosely.

Fasten off A, leaving a long loose end. (The long loose end at beg and end of each row will form fringe.)

1st row Using one strand A and leaving a long loose end, insert hook in first ch, yo and draw a loop through—called *join yarn with a sl st*—, ch1, 1sc in same place as sl st, 1sc in each of rem 103ch. Turn. (104sc)

Fasten off A, leaving a long loose end.

2nd row Using one strand B and leaving a long loose end, join yarn with a sl st in first sc, ch1, 1sc in same place as sl st, 1sc in each of rem 103sc. Turn. Fasten off B, leaving a long loose end.

Cont in this way, starting every row with a new strand of yarn, leaving long loose ends at each end, and working in sc stripes as foll:

1 row more in B, using one strand.

2 rows C, using two strands of yarn held tog.

or make this!

For the wider version of the striped mohair scarf (shown on page 33), work the stripes as for the main scarf, then work eight more rows in stripes as follows:

2 rows C, using two strands.

1 row Rowan *Summer Tweed* in lilac (shade 501), using one strand.

2 rows C, using two strands held tog.

2 rows B, using one strand.

1 row A, using one strand. Fasten off.

Then weave two strands of Rowan *Linen Print* (shade 347) through the two stripes worked in *Summer Tweed*. Tie fringe at the ends as for the main scarf, but dividing strands into seven groups, and trimming to 4in/10cm.

1 row D, using one strand.

2 rows C, using two strands of yarn held tog.

2 rows B, using one strand.

1 row A, using one strand.

Fasten off.

finishing touches

Using a yarn needle and two strands E, weave yarn from end to end of scarf through sts of row worked with yarn D, leaving long loose ends in fringe.

Fringe

At each end of scarf, divide fringe strands into four groups of strands and knot each group tog close to scarf edge. Then trim fringe to 3in/7.5cm long.

loopy scarf

This loopy scarf is so much fun to make that you're sure to want to make it in different colors for different outfits, or as gifts for friends and family. The big loops are merely strands of yarn extended out from the simple single crochet stitches that are worked back and forth in short rows. They are quick to work and you'll pick up the technique in no time at all. Crocheted in superthick wool yarn, the scarf makes a snug winter warmer. I am dying to try it out in various types of novelty yarns—a fur one would be fun—or in mixtures of smooth and knobbly yarns. You can make the scarf as long as you like by just adding more rows.

here's how...

The narrow loopy scarf (see opposite page) is just one stitch narrower than the wide version (see page 37). Before you decide which width to make, work about six rows of each to see which one you like best. It's a good way to practice the loop stitch as well. Don't waste your yarn though: unravel the samples and reuse the yarn in the final scarf.

how big is it?
Wide loopy scarf: The finished scarf measures approximately 3¹/₂in/9cm wide x 55in/138cm long.
Narrow loopy scarf: The finished scarf measures approximately 3in/7.5cm wide x 58in/146cm long.

which stitches?
Single-crochet loop stitch

how much yarn?
Wide loopy scarf
MC = superchunky bicolor wool yarn in main color
   2 x 3¹/₂oz/100g balls Rowan *Big Wool*
   (black and gray—shade no. 11—or chosen color)
CC = superchunky bicolor wool yarn in contrasting color
   1 x 3¹/₂oz/100g ball Rowan *Big Wool*
   (off-white and gray—shade no. 13—or chosen color)
Narrow loopy scarf
MC = superchunky bicolor wool yarn in main color
   1 x 3¹/₂oz/100g ball Rowan *Big Wool*
   (black and gray—shade no. 11—or chosen color)
CC = superchunky bicolor wool yarn in contrasting color
   2 x 3¹/₂oz/100g balls Rowan *Big Wool*
   (off-white and gray—shade no. 13—or chosen color)
(*See page 124 for yarn tips*)

which hook?
12.00mm (US size O/P-15) crochet hook

what gauge?
Approximately 6¹/₂ sts and 5¹/₂ rows to 4in/10cm measured over loop patt using 12.00mm (US size O/P-15) hook.

before you start
- There is no need to check your gauge before beginning the project, as an exact scarf size is not essential.
- *For crochet abbreviations, turn to page 127.*

wide loopy scarf

make the foundation chain
The Wide Loopy Scarf (see page 37) is made up of two identical pieces that are joined tog end to end.
First piece
Using a 12.00mm (US size O/P-15) hook and CC, ch7.
1st patt row Insert hook in 2nd ch from hook, then with yarn around index finger as usual pick up yarn behind finger instead of in front of it and draw a loop through while keeping a 2¹/₂in/6.5cm long loop around index finger, drop loop off finger (but keep loop extended at back of work), yo and draw a loop through both loops on hook to complete sc in usual way—called *loop-sc* or *lp-sc*—, work 1lp-sc in each of rem ch. Turn. (6 sts)
2nd patt row Ch1, work 1lp-sc in each lp-sc. Turn.
Rep last row 4 times more. (There are now 3 loop rows on each side of piece.)
Break off CC.
Using MC, rep 2nd patt row until piece measures 27¹/₂in/69cm from foundation-ch edge—

approximately 32 rows MC (16 loop rows on each side of piece). Fasten off.

Second piece
Make in exactly same way as first piece.

finishing touches
Aligning two pieces of scarf, stitch tog along edges of last row. Weave in any loose ends.

narrow loopy scarf

make the foundation chain
The Narrow Loopy Scarf (see above right) is made up of two identical pieces that are joined tog end to end.

First piece
Using a 12.00mm (US size O/P-15) hook and CC, ch6.
1st patt row Work as for 1st patt row of Wide Loopy Scarf. Turn. (5 sts)
2nd patt row Work as for 2nd patt row of Wide Loopy Scarf.
Rep last row 4 times more. (There are now 3 loop rows on each side of piece.)
Break off CC.
Rep 2nd patt row to form patt **and at the same time** work in stripes as foll:
[6 rows MC, 6 rows CC] twice.
6 rows MC.
4 rows CC.
Fasten off.
Second piece
Make in exactly same way as first piece.

finishing touches
Aligning two pieces of scarf, stitch tog along edges of last row. Weave in any loose ends.

narrow loopy scarf colorways
The Narrow Loopy Scarf (see above) is worked in the same colors as the wide version. For an alternative colorway (see below), work the pattern with the following stripe sequence: 6 rows of white and gray *Big Wool*, 4 rows of a variegated superthick yarn, [8 rows *Big Wool*, 4 rows variegated yarn] twice, 6 rows *Big Wool*.

medallion scarves

If you are new to crochet, you will enjoy working traditional afghan medallions— they have a timeless appeal. If you make them for a scarf, rather than the usual blanket, you can finish the project in a fraction of the time. There are three medallions to choose from. Beginners can start with the Crosses Scarf (see right). Each of the medallions for this scarf is worked in just two quick rounds to make a stylish narrow scarf. The squares for the Diamonds Scarf on page 43 are worked in three rounds, and those for the Circles Scarf (see left) in four rounds. Using a cotton yarn gives a contemporary feel to this traditional design.

here's how...

There are three scarves to choose from. The Crosses scarf shown on page 41 uses the smallest medallion; the Diamonds scarf on the opposite page uses the medium-size medallion; and the Circles Scarf on page 40 uses the largest medallion.

how big is it?

Crosses scarf: When hanging, the finished scarf measures approximately 3¼in/8.5cm wide x 85in/216cm long.

Diamonds scarf: When hanging, the finished scarf measures approximately 3¾in/9.5cm wide x 61in/155cm long.

Circles scarf: When hanging, the finished scarf measures approximately 5½in/14cm wide x 62½in/159cm long.

(For size of medallions, see What Gauge? on page 44)

which stitches?

Crosses scarf
- Double crochet (dc)

Diamonds scarf
- Double crochet (dc)
- Single crochet (sc)

or make this!

The square medallions used for these scarves are usually used to make afghans, so you can turn this pattern into a lightweight throw by working lots more of them. For a winter warmer, make the motifs using a 15.00mm (US size Q) hook and a superthick yarn such as Rowan *Big Wool*.

- Half double crochet (hdc)

Circles scarf
- Double crochet (dc)
- Treble crochet (tr)
- Half double crochet (hdc)
- Single crochet (sc)

how much yarn?

Crosses scarf

A = lightweight silk and cotton blend yarn in first contrasting color

> 1 x 1¾oz/50g hank Rowan *Summer Tweed*
> (off-white—shade no. 524—or chosen color)

B = medium-weight cotton yarn in second contrasting color

> 2 x 1¾oz/50g balls Rowan *All Seasons Cotton*
> (deep navy—shade no. 164—or chosen color)

Diamonds scarf

A = lightweight silk and cotton blend yarn in first contrasting color

> 1 x 1¾oz/50g hank Rowan *Summer Tweed*
> (lime—shade no. 527—or chosen color)

B = lightweight silk and cotton blend yarn in second contrasting color

> 1 x 1¾oz/50g hank Rowan *Summer Tweed*
> (turquoise—shade no. 512—or chosen color)

C = medium-weight cotton yarn in third contrasting color

> 2 x 1¾oz/50g balls Rowan *All Seasons Cotton*
> (deep navy—shade no. 164—or chosen color)

Circles scarf

A = lightweight silk and cotton blend yarn in first contrasting color

> 1 x 1¾oz/50g hank Rowan *Summer Tweed*
> (lime—shade no. 527—or chosen color)

B = lightweight silk and cotton blend yarn in second contrasting color

1 x 1³⁄₄oz/50g hank Rowan *Summer Tweed*
(turquoise—shade no. 512—or chosen color)
C = medium-weight cotton yarn in third
contrasting color
2 x 1³⁄₄oz/50g balls Rowan *All Seasons Cotton*
(deep navy—shade no. 164—or chosen color)
D = medium-weight cotton yarn in fourth
contrasting color
1 x 1³⁄₄oz/50g ball Rowan *All Seasons Cotton*
(pale lime—shade no. 197—or chosen color)
(*See page 124 for yarn tips*)

which hook?

10.00mm (US size N-13) crochet hook

what gauge?

Crosses scarf
Each medallion measures 3³⁄₄in/9.5cm square using
10.00mm (US size N-13) hook.

Diamonds scarf
Each medallion measures 4¹⁄₂in/11.5cm square using
10.00mm (US size N-13) hook.

Circles scarf
Each medallion measures 7in/18cm square using
10.00mm (US size N-13) hook.

before you start

- There is no need to check your gauge before
  beginning, as an exact size is not essential for
  a scarf.
- To avoid having to weave in a loose end at center
  of each medallion when finishing the scarf, work
  over the loose end when working the first round.
  To do this, wrap the strand of yarn clockwise in a
  circle behind the foundation-chain ring before
  beginning the first round. Then work the stitches
  of the first round over it.
- When fastening off the crochet at the end of a
  motif, leave a long loose end to use to sew the
  motifs together.
- *For crochet abbreviations, turn to page 127.*

crosses scarf

make the foundation ring

Using a 10.00mm (US size N-13) hook and A, ch3 and
join with a sl st in first ch to form a ring.
1st rnd (RS) Using A, ch3 to count as first dc, 2dc in
ring, *ch2, 3dc in ring; rep from * twice more, ch2,
break off A and using B join with a sl st in 3rd of ch3.
(Do not turn at end of rnds, but work with RS
always facing.)
2nd rnd Using B, ch3, 1dc in each of next 2dc, *[2dc,
ch4, 2dc] all in next ch2-sp, 1dc in each of next 3dc;
rep from * twice more, [2dc, ch4, 2dc] all in next ch2-
sp, join with a sl st in 3rd of ch3.
Fasten off.
Make 16 more medallions in same way.

finishing touches

Sew medallions together in a row. Knot rem loose
ends together in pairs and weave into work.

diamonds scarf

make the foundation ring

Using a 10.00mm (US size N-13) hook and A, ch3 and
join with a sl st in first ch to form a ring.
1st rnd (RS) Using A, ch3 to count as first dc, 15dc in
ring, break off A and using B join with a sl st in 3rd of
ch3. (Do not turn at end of rnds, but work with RS
always facing.)
2nd rnd Using B, ch1, 1sc in same place as sl st, *skip
1dc, 5hdc in next dc, skip next dc, 1sc in next dc; rep
from * 3 times more omitting sc at end of last rep,
join with a sl st in first sc. Fasten off B.
3rd rnd Using C, join with sl st in center hdc of any
5hdc-group, ch1, 1sc in same place as sl st, *7dc in
next sc (after skipping rem 2hdc of 5hdc-group), 1sc
in center hdc of next 5hdc group; rep from * 3 times
more omitting 1sc at end of last rep, join with a sl st
in first sc. Fasten off.

Make five more medallions in same way. Then make five medallions exactly the same, but using B for foundation ring and 1st rnd, and A for 2nd rnd.

finishing touches

Sew medallions together in a row, alternating two colorways. Weave in ends as for Crosses Scarf.

circles scarf

make the foundation ring

Using a 10.00mm (US size N-13) hook and A, ch4 and join with a sl st in first ch to form a ring.

1st rnd (RS) Using A, ch3 to count as first dc, 15dc in ring, break off A and using B join with a sl st in 3rd of ch3. (Do not turn at end of rnds, but work with RS always facing.)

2nd rnd Using B, ch5, *1dc in next dc, ch2; rep from * to end of rnd, break off B and using C join with a sl st in 3rd of ch5.

3rd rnd Using C, ch6, 1tr in same place as sl st, *ch2, 1dc in next dc, ch2, 1hdc in next dc, ch2, 1dc in next dc, ch2, [1tr, ch2, 1tr] all in next dc; rep from * twice more, ch2, 1dc in next dc, ch2, 1hdc in next dc, ch2, 1dc in next dc, ch2, join with a sl st in 4th of ch6.

4th rnd Using C, 3sc in first ch2-sp, *1sc in next tr, 2sc in next sp, 1sc in next dc, 2sc in next sp, 1sc in next hdc, 2sc in next sp, 1sc in next dc, 2sc in next sp, 1sc in next tr, 3sc in next sp; rep from * twice more, 1sc in next tr, 2sc in next sp, 1sc in next dc, 2sc in next sp, 1sc in next hdc, 2sc in next sp, 1sc in next dc, 2sc in next sp, join with a sl st in first sc. Fasten off.

Make three more medallions in same way. Then make four medallions exactly the same, but using D instead of A for foundation ring and 1st rnd.

finishing touches

Sew medallions together in a row, alternating two colorways. Weave in ends as for Crosses Scarf.

cross, diamond, and circle medallions
The cross medallion above has been enlarged to show the detail. For the size of this square and the diamond (see below) and circle (see bottom) medallions, see gauge opposite.

cotton scarf with beads

Worked in rows of simple single crochet using a soft cotton yarn, this bead-trimmed scarf is comfortable for fall, winter, and spring. Beads and huge-hook crochet are made for each other. Whether you're into small, subtle, delicate beads or big, bold, chunky ones, you can always find a huge-hook texture that will complement them perfectly. Rummaging through beads in a big bead store in central London is one of my favorite pastimes. There is usually some excuse to take me there, but I inevitably walk away with some extra beads that were not on my original list. Why not pick the beads for this scarf before you choose the yarn colors, so you can match the stripes to your delicious beads.

here's how...

If you want to make a neat chain along the foundation-chain edge of your scarf, work the first row of single crochet into the back loop of each chain (see page 31 for how to do this).

how big is it?
The finished scarf measures approximately 4¹/₄in/10.5cm wide x 64in/160cm long, excluding beaded fringe.

which stitches?
Single crochet (sc)

how much yarn?
MC = medium-weight cotton yarn in main color
2 x 1³/₄oz/50g balls Rowan *All Seasons Cotton* (off-white—shade no. 178—or chosen color)
A = lightweight silk and cotton blend yarn in first contrasting color
small amount of Rowan *Summer Tweed* (raspberry—shade no. 528—or chosen color)
B = medium-weight cotton yarn in second contrasting color
small amount of Rowan *All Seasons Cotton* (coral—shade no. 183—or chosen color)
(*See page 124 for yarn tips*)

which hook?
10.00mm (US size N-13) crochet hook

what gauge?
8 sts and 11 rows to 4in/10cm measured over sc stripes using 10.00mm (US size N-13) hook.

any extras?
10 flat round beads (coin-shaped), ¹/₂in/12mm in diameter, or beads of your choice

before you start
- There is no need to check your gauge before beginning, as an exact size is not essential for a scarf.
- Instead of buying a whole ball of A and B, you can use your own yarn scraps for the contrasting stripes on this scarf. Or, if you do buy a whole ball each of A and B, you can make a second scarf to use up the leftovers, making A and B the main colors and MC the simple stripes.
- For a neat color change between the stripes, change to the new color with the last yarn over of the previous row as instructed (see page 89).
- *For crochet abbreviations, turn to page 127.*

make the foundation chain
The scarf is worked from end to end instead of from side to side in the usual way.
Using a 10.00mm (US size N-13) hook and MC, ch129 loosely.
1st row Using MC, 1sc in 2nd ch from hook, 1sc in each of rem 127ch. Turn. (128sc)
2nd row Using MC, ch1, 1sc in each sc to last sc, insert hook in last sc, yo and draw a loop through, break off MC and using A, yo and draw through both loops on hook to complete last sc. Turn.
3rd row Using A, 1sc in each sc, breaking off A and changing to MC with last yo of last sc. Turn.
Cont in sc, changing to a new color with last yo of last sc of previous row, and work in stripes as foll:
3 rows MC.
1 row B.
2 rows MC.
1 row A, changing to MC with last yo of last sc.
Edging
Work next row and cont the edging around edge of scarf as foll:

Next rnd Using MC, 1sc in each sc to last sc, 3sc in last sc; then with same side still facing, work 6sc evenly along end of scarf and 3sc in corner; cont along long edge of scarf (foundation-ch edge) and work 1sc in each ch, then 3sc in next corner; work 6sc along other end of scarf, 2sc in corner and join with a sl st in first sc of rnd.

finishing touches

Weave in any loose ends.

Twisted cords for fringe

Make five twisted cords for each end of scarf as foll: Cut five strands of MC, each 24in/60cm long, and make a 7in/18cm long twisted cord with each strand, knotting only one end of cords and leaving folded end unknotted (see page 123 for how to make twisted cords).

If your beads have small holes, attach knotted ends of five cords to each end of scarf, then attach beads (see caption right).

If your beads have a hole big enough for passing twisted cord through, pass folded end of first cord through center of edge of scarf at one end, open loop at fold, pass cord through loop, and pull tight. Attach four other cords at equal intervals along end of scarf. Then cut off knot at end of first cord and, keeping twist pinched tog, pass it through bead. Reknot with bead approximately 3½in/9cm from edge of scarf. Secure a bead to each of rem cords in same way.

attaching small-holed beads

If your beads have only small holes, like the ones above, shown on an alternative colorway of the scarf, you can tie the beads to the ends of the twisted cords, using sewing thread that matches the beads.

pompom scarves

The pompoms add a little spark to these narrow chenille scarves worked with the very biggest crochet hook around—it's 20 millimeters in diameter (US size S). The giant hook creates a texture that looks like a complicated lace stitch, but it's really just rows of simple double crochet worked with two strands of chunky chenille held together. Only three rows wide, the scarves are crocheted from end to end instead of from side to side in the usual way. They drape so beautifully that I am going to make several for myself in different colors and widths (not all with pompoms). Great to wear for a layered look.

here's how...

There are four lengths to choose from for these scarves. Before deciding how many chains to start with, find a scarf in your wardrobe that you like the length of and choose the length closest to this.

how big is it?

The finished scarves measure approximately 4¹/₄in/10.5cm wide and can be worked in four different lengths—40[60¹/₂:76¹/₂:90¹/₄]in/ 100[151.5:191.5:225.5]cm, excluding the pompoms.

which stitches?

Double crochet (dc)

how much yarn?

Green and blue scarves

MC = chunky cotton chenille yarn in main color
1[2: 2] x 3¹/₂oz/100g balls Rowan *Chunky Cotton Chenille* (light sage green—shade no. 393; or blue—shade no. 394)

Green scarf pompoms

A = chunky cotton chenille yarn in first contrasting color
small amount of Rowan *Chunky Cotton Chenille* (blue—shade no. 394—or chosen color)

B = lightweight silk and cotton blend yarn in second contrasting color
small amount of Rowan *Summer Tweed* (lime—shade no. 527—or chosen color)

Blue scarf pompoms

A = chunky cotton chenille yarn in first contrasting color
small amount of Rowan *Chunky Cotton Chenille* (light sage green—shade no. 393—or chosen color)

B = lightweight silk and cotton blend yarn in second contrasting color

small amount of Rowan *Summer Tweed* (lime—shade no. 527—or chosen color)
(*See page 124 for yarn tips*)

which hook?

20.00mm (US size S) crochet hook

any extras?

- Strong cotton yarn that matches MC, for tying pompoms when making them
- Strong sewing thread that matches MC, for sewing on pompoms

what gauge?

3¹/₂ sts and 3¹/₂ rows to 4in/10cm measured over dc using two strands MC and 20.00mm (US size S) hook.

before you start

- There is no need to check your gauge before beginning, as an exact scarf size is not essential.
- To create a chain edge along the foundation-chain edge of the scarf, work the first row of dc into the back loop of each chain (see page 31).
- *For crochet abbreviations, turn to page 127.*

green scarf

make the foundation chain

The scarf is worked from end to end instead of from side to side in the usual way.

Using a 20.00mm (US size S) hook and two strands MC held tog, ch37[55:69:81] loosely.

1st row 1dc in 4th ch from hook, 1dc in each of rem 33[51:65:77]ch. Turn.

2nd row Ch3 (to count as first dc), skip first dc and work 1dc in next dc, 1dc in each of rem dc, ending

with 1dc in 3rd of ch3. Turn. (35[53:67:79] sts)
3rd row As 2nd row.
Fasten off.

finishing touches

Weave in any loose ends.
Pompoms
Make six pompoms in total—three for each end of scarf—each 1³⁄₈in/3.5cm in diameter. Follow instructions right, wrapping yarns A, B, and MC around cardboard pompom-maker in that order. Stitch three pompoms to each end of scarf with a matching sewing thread.

blue scarf

make the foundation chain

Make the Blue Scarf exactly as for the Green Scarf.

finishing touches

Gather both ends of scarf with a single strand of MC. Weave in any loose ends.
Dangling pompoms
Make six pompoms in total—three for each end of scarf—each 1³⁄₈in/3.5cm in diameter. Follow instructions right, wrapping yarns A, B, and MC around cardboard pompom-maker in that order. Then make six twisted cords in total—four 5in/13cm long and two 6¹⁄₂in/16.5cm long (see page 123 for how to make twisted cords). Leave folded ends of twisted cords unknotted.
Using a matching sewing thread, stitch knotted end of each cord to a pompom, hiding knot inside pompom strands.
Join one long and two short dangling pompoms to each end of scarf with a single strand of MC.

make quick pompoms!

You may have an excellent pompom-making tool—and there are several types to choose from—but if, like me, you find the one you have slows the process down, try this technique. Cut a 5–6in/13–15cm long strip of cardboard as wide as the desired diameter of your pompom (1³⁄₈in/3.5cm for the Pompom Scarves). Fold the cardboard in half widthwise and poke a hole through the center of both layers near the fold. Then cut through the center of the strip to the holes as shown (A). Cut a length of strong yarn for tying the pompom and thread it through the holes. Next, wrap the yarn round and round the cardboard until there's enough yarn for a nice plump pompom (B). Slide the other end of the tying strand through the cut slots and knot tightly around the pompom. Cut through the pompom yarn at the top and bottom, passing the scissor blades between the layers (C). Slide the pompom off the cardboard and trim the shape to neatly round it (D).

string shopper

One of the best things about working with huge hooks is that you can form chunky stitches with string and twine. Made using green and olive garden twine and blue and turquoise packaging string, this sturdy crochet bag is perfect for casual weekend shopping. You should be able to find string in all sorts of colors, so get creative and choose your own striped color scheme. Or, work the bag in a solid color and use a contrasting color for the edging. Although the bag is worked in simple single crochet, you need to keep track of the increases as you work, so choose this as your third or fourth project if you are an absolute beginner.

here's how...

This String Shopper is made in three pieces; there are two side panels and a single piece for the front and back. The front and back piece is an oval shape, so the single crochet is worked in rounds instead of rows. Increases are worked at each end of the oval to create the rounded ends (see page 24 for instructions for how to work simple increases). By placing markers as explained in the pattern instructions you will be able to position the increases with ease.

how big is it?
The finished bag measures approximately 10in/25.5cm tall x 15in/37.5cm wide x 3in/7.5cm deep.

which stitches?
Single crochet (sc)

how much "yarn"?
MC = twine in main color
    330yd/300m of dark green garden twine
A = twine in first contrasting color
    165yd/150m of olive green garden twine
B = string in second contrasting color
    44yd/40m of light turquoise general-purpose polypropylene string
C = string in third contrasting color
    87yd/80m of mid blue general-purpose polypropylene string
D = string in fourth contrasting color
    44yd/40m of mid turquoise general-purpose polypropylene string

which hooks?
8.00mm, 9.00mm, and 10.00mm (US sizes L-11, M, and N-13) crochet hooks

choosing string
The olive and dark green shades (see above) used for the String Shopper are garden twine purchased from a big garden store. The remaining shades are general-purpose string available in home improvement stores.

what gauge?

7 sts and 8$\frac{1}{2}$ rows to 4in/10cm measured over sc using two strands MC held tog and 10.00mm (US size N-13) hook.

any extras?

Green plastic-coated garden wire, 1mm in diameter (optional)

before you start

- Make a swatch of single crochet to check your gauge before beginning. If your string is finer than the one used here, you may need to use three strands instead of two to get the right gauge. (See page 25 for information about checking gauge.)
- The front and back of the bag are worked in a single oval-shaped piece and the stripe pattern is worked in rounds with the WS always facing. At the end of each round the color used is fastened off, then the next round is started by joining on the new color in the center of one side so the joins will be positioned at the bottom of the bag. Join in the new color in a slightly different place in each round.
- *For crochet abbreviations, turn to page 127.*

make the foundation chain

The bag is made in three pieces—one piece for back and front, and two side panels.

Front and back (one piece)

Using a 10.00mm (US size N-13) hook and two strands A held tog, ch13.

Beg stripe patt as foll:

1st rnd (WS) Using two strands A, 5sc in 2nd ch from hook, 1sc in each of next 10ch, 5sc in last ch, then cont around other side of foundation ch and

work 1sc in each of next 10ch, join with a sl st in first sc. (30sc) Fasten off.

Do not turn at end of rnds, but work with WS always facing.

Cont as foll:

2nd rnd Using two strands MC, join with a sl st in a sc at center of one side of piece, ch1, 1sc in same place as sl st, *1sc in each sc until 5sc at end is reached, then lay a strand of contrasting yarn across work to mark position of next st—called *place marker*—, 1sc in first of 5sc group, 2sc in next sc, 3sc in next sc, 2sc in next sc, 1sc in next sc, place marker*; rep from * to *, 1sc in each sc to end of rnd, join with sl st in first sc. (38sc)

Fasten off.

3rd rnd Using two strands B, join with a sl st in a sc at center of one side of piece, ch1, 1sc in same place as sl st, 1sc in each sc until first marker is reached, *place marker, 2sc in next sc, 1sc in each of next 2sc, 2sc in next sc, 1sc in next sc, 2sc in next sc, 1sc in each of next 2sc, 2sc in next sc (next marker now reached), place marker*, 1sc in each sc until next marker is reached; rep from * to *, 1sc in each sc to

end of rnd, join with sl st in first sc. (46sc)
Fasten off.
Work next rnd without inc, but still placing markers, as foll:

4th rnd Using two strands MC, join with a sl st in a sc at center of one side, ch1, 1sc in same place as sl st, [1sc in each sc to next marker, place marker] 4 times, 1sc in each sc to end of rnd, join with sl st in first sc. Fasten off.

5th rnd Using two strands A, join with a sl st in a sc at center of one side, ch1, 1sc in same place as sl st, 1sc in each sc until first marker is reached, *place marker, [1sc in next sc, 2sc in next sc] 6 times, 1sc in next sc (next marker now reached), place marker*, 1sc in each sc until next marker is reached; rep from * to *, 1sc in each sc to end of rnd, join with sl st in first sc. (58sc)
Fasten off.

6th rnd Using two strands MC, as 4th rnd.
Fasten off.

7th rnd Using two strands C, join with a sl st in a sc at center of one side, ch1, 1sc in same place as sl st, 1sc in each sc until first marker is reached, *place marker, [2sc in next sc, 1sc in each of next 2sc] 6 times, 2sc in next sc (next marker now reached), place marker*, 1sc in each sc until next marker is reached; rep from * to *, 1sc in each sc to end of rnd, join with sl st in first sc. (72sc)
Fasten off.

8th rnd Using two strands MC, as 4th rnd.
Fasten off.

9th rnd Using two strands A, join with a sl st in a sc at center of one side, ch1, 1sc in same place as sl st, 1sc in each sc until first marker is reached, *place marker, [1sc in each of next 3sc, 2sc in next sc] 6 times, 1sc in each of next 2sc (next marker now reached), place marker*, 1sc in each sc until next marker is reached; rep from * to *, 1sc in each sc to end of rnd, join with sl st in first sc. (84sc) Fasten off.

10th rnd Using two strands MC, as 4th rnd.
Fasten off.

11th rnd Using two strands D, as 4th rnd.
Fasten off.

12th rnd Using two strands MC, join with a sl st in a sc at center of one side, ch1, 1sc in same place as sl st, 1sc in each sc until first marker is reached, *place marker, 1sc in each of next 8sc, [2sc in next sc, 1sc in each of next 4sc] 3 times, 2sc in next sc, 1sc in each of next 8sc (next marker now reached), place marker*, 1sc in each sc until next marker is reached; rep from * to *, 1sc in each sc to end of rnd, join with sl st in first sc. (92sc)
Fasten off.

13th rnd Using two strands A, as 4th rnd.
Fasten off.

14th rnd Using two strands MC, as 4th rnd.
Fasten off.

15th rnd Using two strands C, join with a sl st in a sc at center of one side, ch1, 1sc in same place as sl st, 1sc in each sc until first marker is reached, *place marker, 1sc in each of next 8sc, 2sc in next sc, 1sc in each of next 5sc, 2sc in next sc, 1sc in each of next 6sc, 2sc in next sc, 1sc in each of next 5sc, 2sc in next sc, 1sc in each of next 8sc (next marker now reached), place marker*, 1sc in each sc until next marker is reached; rep from * to *, 1sc in each sc to end of rnd, join with sl st in first sc. (100sc)
Fasten off.

16th rnd Using two strands MC, as 4th rnd.
Fasten off.

Side panels (make 2 alike)
Using 10.00mm (US size N-13 hook) and two strands MC held tog, ch4.

1st row 1sc in 2nd ch from hook, 1sc in each of rem 2ch. Turn. (3sc)

2nd row Ch1, 1sc in each sc. Turn.
Rep last row 9 times more.
Work edging as foll:

Next rnd Ch1, 1sc in each of first 2sc, 3sc in last sc, then cont around side of piece and work 1sc in each row end, 3sc in corner foundation ch, 1sc in next foundation ch, 3sc in next foundation ch, 1sc in each

row end to last row end, 3sc in last row end, join with a sl st to first sc of row.
Fasten off.

finishing touches

Fold bag in half and mark position of foldline on each side. Pin each side panel to front and back piece with WS tog and matching center of bottom of panel with marked center of bag.

Using 10.00mm (US size N-13) hook and two strands MC held tog, and with side panel facing, join panel to bag with sl sts, working each sl st through a sc on both layers.

Handles (make 2 alike)
Using a 8.00mm (US size L-11) hook and one strand MC, ch18.

1st row 1sc in 2nd ch from hook, 1sc in each of rem 16ch. Turn. (17sc)

Change to 9.00mm (US size M) hook and cont as foll:

2nd row Ch1, 1sc in each sc. Turn. (17sc)

Join foundation-ch edge to top of last row as foll:

Joining row Holding handle with working string at right, fold it half lengthwise by bringing foundation-ch edge up in back so that it is level with top of sc of previous row, then work sc through both layers, inserting hook under both loops at top of each sc of previous row and through corresponding foundation ch with each sc.

Fasten off.

Stitch each handle in place in center of top of bag, with handle ends 4in/10cm apart and securing them to WS of sc in last rnd.

If desired, stiffen curved edge of bag by inserting green garden wire through sts of last rnd and fastening off wire ends safely and securely so they won't poke out.

crochet in the round
The single oval piece that forms the front and back of the String Shopper is created by working the crochet in rounds and using increases to produce the curves.

single-crochet bags

These wool bags were inspired by a finely crocheted bag carried by my smartly dressed 12-year-old niece Meg on sightseeing day-trips around London last year. I have done three very different versions of this simple basic shape for you to choose from. The Beaded Bag on the left has two short handles, is edged with beads, and can be crocheted in any color you like. The Striped Bag on page 64 (and with a detail, right) has a closing tab and a short double twisted-cord shoulder strap. The V-stitch Bag on page 66 has a long shoulder strap tipped with beaded tassels.

here's how...

Once you've followed one of the bag patterns, you'll be able to adapt it to your own versions—plain, striped, or patterned. Experienced crocheters can use the patterns to make coin purses with zippers, by using a finer yarn and a smaller hook.

how big is it?

Beaded bag: The finished bag measures approximately 6½in/16cm wide x 8½in/21cm tall.
Striped bag: The finished bag measures approximately 6½in/16cm wide x 8½in/21cm tall.
V-stitch bag: The finished bag measures approximately 6¾in/17cm wide x 8½in/21cm tall.

which stitches?

- Single crochet (sc)
- V-stitch pattern (V-stitch bag only)

how much yarn?

Beaded bag
Chunky wool yarn
   2 x 3½oz/100g balls Rowan *Polar*
   (fuchsia—shade no. 651—or chosen color)

or make this!

The pattern for this bag can easily be adapted for a bigger bag. Make the Beaded or Striped Bag first and you'll figure out at once how to make a bigger bag—just make more foundation chains at the start. For a big tote, however, avoid wool and use two or more strands of a cotton yarn instead, to produce a really strong bag.

Striped bag
MC = chunky wool yarn in main color
   1 x 3½oz/100g ball Colinette *Point 5*
   in chosen color
CC = chunky variegated wool yarn in contrasting color
   1 x 3½oz/100g ball Colinette *Point 5*
   in chosen color

V-stitch bag
MC = chunky wool yarn in main color
   2 x 3½oz/100g balls Rowan *Polar*
   (charcoal—shade no. 647—or chosen color)
A = chunky wool yarn in first contrasting color
   1 x 3½oz/100g ball Rowan *Polar*
   (white—shade no. 645—or chosen color)
B = lightweight silk and cotton blend yarn in second contrasting color
   small amount of Rowan *Summer Tweed*
   (raspberry—shade no. 528—or chosen color)
(See page 124 for yarn tips)

which hooks?

Beaded bag: 9.00mm and 12.00mm (US size M and O/P-15) crochet hooks
Striped bag: 10.00mm (US size N-13) crochet hook
V-stitch bag: 12.00mm (US size O/P-15) crochet hook
(See page 127 for hook comparison chart)

any extras?

- **Beaded bag:** 13 round beads, approximately ⅜in/1cm in diameter
- **V-stitch bag:** 8 beads, approximately ½in/12mm in diameter
- **All bags:** strong thread for sewing on straps; plus matching fabric and sewing thread for bag lining (instructions for lining bags are given on page 121)

what gauge?

Beaded bag: 8 sts and 9 rows to 4in/10cm measured over sc using 12.00mm (US size O/P-15) hook.
Striped bag: 8 sts and 9 rows to 4in/10cm measured over sc using 10.00mm (US size N-13) hook.
V-stitch bag: 8 sts and 9 rows to 4in/10cm measured over V-st patt using 12.00mm (US size O/P-15) hook.

before you start

- There is no need to check your gauge before beginning, as an exact bag size is not essential.
- When making the V-stitch bag, keep track of where the rounds begin and end to work the bag correctly. To do this, before starting a round, place a contrasting strand of yarn across the crochet fabric from front to back, close up against the loop on the hook and *above the working yarn*. Start to work the first st of the following round, catching the marker in position. The marker marks the start of the round and is caught under the top of the first stitch of the round.
- *For crochet abbreviations, turn to page 127.*

beaded bag

make the foundation chain

The Beaded Bag on page 60 is worked in the round in one piece, but starts with a straight foundation chain instead of a ring of chain.

Using a 12.00mm (US size O/P-15) hook and two strands of yarn held tog, ch14.

1st rnd (RS) Inserting hook under only one lp of each ch (see page 19), work 1sc in 2nd ch from hook, 1sc in each of rem 12ch, then cont around other side of foundation ch and inserting hook in other side of each ch, work 1sc in each of 13ch. (26sc)

sew on the beads like this!

To sew the beads on the Beaded Bag, first thread a yarn needle with a long length of a single strand of the yarn used for the bag. Then secure the yarn to the wrong side of the top edge of the bag at a side-fold and bring it out in the middle of a "chain" at the top of a single crochet stitch. Thread the 13 beads onto the yarn. Slide the first bead up to the bag and using a separate length of yarn (the "couching" yarn), secure the beads as shown. Position each bead on top of a single crochet stitch and space the beads apart so there is one single crochet between beads. When you are finished, secure both ends of yarn to the inside of the bag.

(Do not turn at end of rnds, but keep RS always facing. Note that the side-folds of the bag will form naturally at each end of the foundation ch as the bag is worked upward.)

Mark end of last rnd with a contrasting yarn to keep track of which side-fold is beg of rnds.

2nd rnd 1sc in each sc.

Rep last rnd until bag measures 8¹⁄₂in/21cm tall (approximately 19 rnds in total), ending at marked side-fold.

Work a sl st in next sc and fasten off.

finishing touches

Weave in any loose ends.

Sew beads to top edge of bag as instructed in tip box on page 63.

Handles (make 2 alike)

Using 9.00mm (US size M) and two strands of yarn held tog, ch31.

1st row Inserting hook into back lp of each ch to make a chained edge (see page 31), work 1 sl st in 2nd ch from hook, 1 sl st in each of rem 29ch. Fasten off.

Using a strong sewing thread, sew one handle to front of bag and one to back of bag, stitching them to inside of bag and 3/4in/2cm from side-folds.

Line bag with matching fabric (see page 121).

striped bag

make the foundation chain

The Striped Bag opposite is worked in the round in one piece, but starts with a straight foundation chain instead of a ring of chain.

Using a 10.00mm (US size N-13) hook and MC, ch14.

1st rnd (RS) Inserting hook through only one lp of each ch (see page 19), work 1sc in 2nd ch from hook, 1sc in each of rem 12ch, then cont around other side of foundation ch and inserting hook in other side of each ch, work 1sc in each of 13ch. (26sc)

(Do not turn at end of rnds, but keep RS always facing. Note that the side-folds of the bag will form naturally at each end of the foundation ch as the bag is worked upward.)

Mark end of last rnd with a contrasting yarn to keep track of which side-fold is beg of rnds.

2nd rnd 1sc in each sc.

3rd rnd As 2nd rnd.

4th rnd 1sc in each sc to within last sc of rnd, 1sc in last sc breaking off MC and changing to CC with last yo of this sc (see page 89 for instructions for how to change colors).

Cont in sc in this way, starting and stopping stripes at side-fold and working stripes as foll:

3 rnds CC.

5 rnds MC.

2 rnds CC.

4 rnds MC.

If necessary, cont in MC until bag measures 8½in/21cm tall, ending at marked side-fold.

Work a sl st in next sc and fasten off.

finishing touches

Weave in any loose ends.

Closing tab

Using a 10.00mm (US size N-13) hook and MC, work a closing tab directly onto top of bag as foll:

1st row Insert hook through top of 6th sc from side-fold at top of back of bag, yo and draw a lp through—called *join with a sl st*—, ch1, 1sc in same place as sl st, 1sc in each of next 2sc. Turn. (3sc)

2nd row Ch1, 1sc in each sc. Turn.

Rep last row 5 times more.

Fasten off.

Cord holder for tab

Cut two strands MC, each 16in/40cm long. With these two strands held tog, make a twisted cord (see page 123). Knot each end of cord so knots are 2¾in/7cm apart. Then trim off excess yarn close to knots. To attach cord holder to front of bag, poke knots through holes in crochet below top 2 rows, positioning cord in center of front with ends 3sc apart. Stitch knots to inside of bag.

Straps

Make two 21½in/55cm long twisted cords for straps. To make cords, cut 51in/130cm lengths of yarn, and use two strands of MC held tog to make one cord and one strand each of CC and MC held tog for other cord (see page 123).

Using strong sewing thread, stitch cord ends to inside of bag at side-folds and ½in/1.5cm below top edge.

Line bag with matching fabric (see page 121).

V-stitch bag

make the foundation chain

The V-stitch Bag opposite is worked in the round in one piece, but starts with a straight foundation chain instead of a ring of chain.

Using a 12.00mm (US size O/P-15) hook and two strands MC, ch14.

Using two strands MC or two strands A throughout, beg bag as foll:

1st rnd (RS) Inserting hook through only one lp of each ch (see page 19), work 1sc in 2nd ch from hook, 1sc in each of rem 12ch, then cont around other side of foundation ch and inserting hook in other side of each ch, work 1sc in each of first 12ch, 2sc in last ch. (27sc)

(Do not turn at end of rnds, but keep RS always facing. Note that the side-folds of the bag will form naturally at each end of the foundation ch as the bag is worked upward.)

Remember to mark beg of each rnd (see Before You Start) in order to keep track of where each rnd begins and ends.

2nd rnd Using MC, 1sc in each sc. (27sc)

3rd rnd As 2nd rnd.

4th rnd *Using MC, 1sc in each of next 2sc changing to A with last yo of 2nd sc and dropping MC at WS, insert hook from front to back through top of sc one row below next sc (in same place sc in previous row was worked), wrap A around hook and draw a lp through, drop A at WS and using MC wrap yarn around hook and draw through 2 lps on hook to complete st—called *long-sc*—*; rep from * to * 8 times more.

5th rnd Using MC, 1sc in each st.

6th rnd *Using MC, 1sc in next sc changing to A with last yo of this st, using A work 1 long-sc in sc one row below next sc changing to MC with last yo of this st, using MC 1sc in next sc*; rep from * to * 8 times more.

7th rnd As 5th rnd.

8th rnd Using MC, 1sc in each of first 2sc, then reposition marker to make next st first st of rnd (this is to keep beg of rnd at side-fold of bag because it moves naturally diagonally to right), *using MC, 1sc in next sc changing to A with last yo of this st, using A work 1 long-sc in sc one row below next sc changing to MC with last yo of this st, using MC 1sc in next sc*; rep from * to * 8 times more.

9th rnd As 5th rnd.

10th rnd Using MC, 1sc in first sc, then reposition marker to make next st first st of rnd, *using MC, 1sc in each of next 2sc changing to A with last yo of 2nd sc, using A work 1 long-sc in sc one row below next sc changing to MC with last yo of this st*; rep from * to * 8 times more.

11th rnd As 5th rnd.

12th rnd As 6th rnd.

13th rnd As 5th rnd.

14th rnd As 10th rnd.

15th rnd As 5th rnd.

16th rnd As 6th rnd.

Break off A.

17th rnd As 5th rnd.

18th rnd Using MC, 1sc in each sc, changing to four strands B with last yo of last sc.

Using four strands B, work next rnd as foll:

19th rnd Using B, 1 sl st in back lp of each sc.

Fasten off.

finishing touches

Weave in any loose ends.

Strap

Make a double-chain cord using two strands MC for each side of cord as foll:

Using a 12.00mm (US size O/P-15) hook and two strands MC, make a slip knot, leaving 8in/20cm long loose ends. Using a separate two strands MC and again leaving long loose ends, draw a lp through slip knot to make first ch. *Using first double strand of MC, ch1, using second double strand of MC, ch1; rep from * alternating from one double strand of MC to the other, until strap measures 38in/96.5cm when stretched. (To make strap quicker, hold one double strand MC over index finger in usual way, and the other over thumb.) Fasten off, leaving 8in/20cm long loose ends at end of strap.

Thread a bead onto each of four strands of yarn at each end of cord. To secure each bead, knot yarn about 1³⁄₄in/4.5cm from end of strap. Trim ends of yarn close to knots.

Using strong sewing thread, stitch strap ends to outside of bag at side-folds.

Line bag with matching fabric (see page 121).

rag handbag

Crocheting with strips of silk douppioni is incredibly satisfying. The "yarn" is quick to make because the fabric tears so easily, and the lustrous colors of the silk are amazing. To form the bold single crochet stitches of this "rag" crochet bag, I used a 15.00mm (US size Q) crochet hook and two strips of the silk held together. The resulting fabric is perfect for a handbag, chunky and sturdy. If making the bag with a gusset seems a bit too advanced for your tastes, you can make two simple "rag" crochet squares for your bag, stitch them together, and add twisted-cord handles, one on each side of the bag.

here's how...

Working with silk strips creates lots of frayed ends. While you're crocheting, ignore the untidiness. Once the bag is completed you can snip off the ends.

how big is it?
The finished bag measures approximately 10^1/$_4$in/25.5cm tall x 12^1/$_2$in/31cm wide x 2^3/$_4$in/6.5cm deep.

which stitches?
Single crochet (sc)

how much "yarn"?
A = silk fabric strips in first contrasting color 3^1/$_4$yd/3m of 44in/112cm wide striped turquoise silk

B = silk fabric strips in second contrasting color 20in/50cm of 44in/112cm wide pale turquoise douppioni silk

C = silk fabric strips in third contrasting color 1yd/90cm of 44in/112cm wide striped mid olive silk

D = silk fabric strips in fourth contrasting color 1^3/$_4$yd/1.4m of 44in/112cm wide light olive douppioni silk

E = silk fabric strips in fifth contrasting color 20in/50cm of 44in/112cm wide lime douppioni silk

F = silk fabric strips in fifth contrasting color 16in/40cm of 44in/112cm wide dark turquoise douppioni silk

which hook?
15.00mm (US size Q) crochet hook

any extras?
- Sewing thread for joining crocheted pieces
- 16in/40cm of 44in/112in wide douppioni silk in chosen color for lining and matching thread

what gauge?
Approximately 4^1/$_2$ sts and 5^1/$_2$ rows to 4in/10cm measured over sc using two fabric strips held tog and 15.00mm (US size Q) hook.

before you start
- Cut or tear the fabric strips about 1^1/$_4$in/3cm wide (see pages 97 and 117 for how to prepare fabric strips).
- *For crochet abbreviations, turn to page 127.*

make the foundation chain
The bag is made in three pieces—a front, a back, and a gusset.

Front and back (both alike)

Using a 15.00mm (US size Q) hook and two strips A held tog, ch15.

Remembering to use two strips of each color throughout, cont as foll:

1st row (WS) Using A, 1sc in 2nd ch from hook, 1sc in each of rem 13ch. Turn. (14sc)

2nd row (RS) Using A, ch1, 1sc in each sc to end. Turn.

3rd row Using A, ch1, 1sc in each sc to last sc, insert hook in last sc, yo and draw a lp through, drop A, then using B, yo and draw through 2 lps on hook to complete last sc. Turn.

Break off A.

4th row Using B, ch1, 1sc in each sc to last sc, insert hook in last sc, yo and draw a lp through, drop B, then using C, yo and draw through 2 lps on hook to complete last sc. Turn.

Using two strips of each color, cont in same way, changing to new color with last yo of last sc of row, **and at the same time** work in sc in stripes as foll: 1 row C, 1 row D, 1 row E, 1 row D, 1 row C, and 1 row D, changing to A with last yo of last row.

Divide for handle

Divide for handle on next row as foll:

11th row (WS) Using A, ch1, 1sc in each of first 5sc, fasten off, skip next 4sc, join A with a sl st to next sc, ch1, 1sc in same place as sl st, 1sc in each of last 4sc. Turn.

12th row Using A, ch1, 1sc in each of first 5sc, ch4, 1sc in each of next 5sc, changing to F with last yo of last sc. Turn.

13th row Using F, ch1, 1sc in each of first 5sc, 1sc in each of next 4ch, 1sc in each of last 5sc, changing to A with last yo of last sc. Turn.

14th row Using A, ch1, 1sc in each sc.

Fasten off.

Do not trim frayed thread ends until bag is stitched tog.

Gusset

Using a 15.00mm (US size Q) hook and two strips A, ch4.

Beg first half of gusset as foll:

1st row Using A, 1sc in 2nd ch from hook, 1sc in each of rem 2ch. Turn. (3sc)

2nd row Using A, ch1, 1sc in each sc. Turn.

Rep last row until piece fits from center of bottom of front, around corner of bag, and up to first row of B (approximately 10 rows A in total). Then cont in sc matching stripes at side of bag and changing to new color as for bag as foll:

1 row B, 1 row C, 1 row D, 1 row E, 1 row D, 1 row C, and 1 row D.

Fasten off.

Turn gusset piece around so that foundation-ch edge is uppermost and join A with a sl st to other side of first foundation ch, ch1, 1sc in same place as sl st, 1sc in each of rem 2ch.

Cont in sc working same number of rows in A as first end of gusset to first row of B.

Then rep stripe sequence from ** to **.

Fasten off.

finishing touches

Weave in any loose ends.

To line bag, use crocheted front, back, and gusset as guides for size of fabric pattern pieces. Allow for a seam allowance of 1/2in/1.5cm all around each lining piece. Cut lining pieces and press seam allowances to WS. Pin each lining piece to WS of corresponding crochet piece and slip stitch in place with sewing thread.

Pin back and front of bag to gusset, matching stripes along sides of bag, and placing lined sides tog. Using strong sewing thread, stitch gusset carefully in place.

Snip off any frayed ends.

If you want to try "rag" crochet, making this roomy shoulder bag is a good starting point. Three strands of chunky chenille are used together for crocheting the main part of the

bag with rag strap

bag to make a firm, dense fabric. Only the strap and gusset, which are worked in one piece, are made in "rag" crochet with strips of douppioni silk. Single crochet stitches are used for all the pieces of the bag, so it is extra quick and easy to make. Pick silk colors to complement the yarn color you've chosen, and prepare the silk strips before you start, winding them into balls.

here's how...

Before you start the Bag with Rag Strap, prepare your "rag" yarn by cutting or tearing strips approximately ³/₄in (2cm) wide. Turn to page 117 for instructions for how to tear or cut fabric strips in the usual way, or to page 97 for a super-quick cutting technique.

how big is it?

The finished bag measures approximately 13in/32.5cm wide x 10¹/₂in/26cm tall x 2in/5cm deep.

which stitches?

Single crochet (sc)

how much yarn?

MC = chunky cotton chenille in main color
  3 x 3¹/₂oz/100g balls Rowan *Chunky Cotton Chenille* (aqua blue—shade no. 392—or chosen color)
A, **B**, and **C** = silk fabric strips in three contrasting colors
  ³/₄yd/70cm of 44in/112cm wide silk douppioni

try this!

- To avoid having to weave in lots of loose ends, when changing colors on the "rag" crochet strap, work your crochet stitches over the ends of the silk strips.

- While crocheting the strap/gusset you'll notice that frayed threads appear. Wait until the bag is complete to trim off these threads.

in each of lilac-gray, lilac, and turquoise or three chosen colors
(*See page 124 for yarn tips*)

which hook?

10.00mm (US size N-13) crochet hook

any extras?

- Large button and sewing thread
- Lining fabric and matching sewing thread (optional)

what gauge?

- 8 sts and 8 rows to 4in/10cm measured over sc using three strands MC held tog and 10.00mm (US size N-13) hook.
- 10 sts and 7¹/₂ rows to 4in/10cm measured over sc (stretched slightly) using A (fabric strip) and 10.00mm (US size N-13) hook.

before you start

- There is no need to check your gauge before beginning, as an exact size is not essential for a bag.
- *For crochet abbreviations, turn to page 127.*

make the foundation chain

The bag is made in three pieces—a front, a back, and a strap/gusset.
Front and back (both alike)
Using a 10.00mm (US size N-13) hook and three strands MC held tog, ch27.
1st row 1sc in 2nd ch from hook, 1sc in each of rem 25ch. Turn. (26sc)
2nd row Ch1, 1sc in each sc to end. Turn.
Rep last row until piece measures 10¹/₂in/26cm from foundation-ch edge—total of approximately 21 rows.

Strap/gusset

The strap also forms the gusset on the bag.

Using a 10.00mm (US size N-13) hook and A, ch6.

1st row 1sc in 2nd ch from hook, 1sc in each of rem 4ch. Turn. (5sc)

2nd row Ch1, 1sc in each sc to end. Turn.

Rep last row 3 times more, changing to B with last yo of last sc.

Break off A.

Cont in sc and work in stripes, changing to new color with last yo of last sc of old color, as foll:

*5 rows B.

5 rows C.

5 rows A.*

Rep from * to * 7 times more.

Then work 5 rows B, 5 rows C.

Fasten off.

finishing touches

Weave in any loose ends.

Sew ends of strap/gusset tog to form a ring.

Positioning strap/gusset seam at center of foundation-ch edge of front of bag and with WS tog, pin strap/gusset to front along two sides and bottom edge. With strap/gusset facing you, using 10.00mm (US size N-13) hook and two strands MC, and starting at top of one side edge, work sc through edge of both layers all around edge of bag, then cont sc along free edge of strap to beg of rnd of sc; join with a sl st in first sc.

Fasten off.

Join strap/gusset to back of bag in same way.

Button loop

Make a 4¹⁄₄in/11cm long twisted cord for button. For cord, cut two 20in/50cm lengths of MC. With these two strands held tog, make a cord as explained on page 123.

crochet

shirt button

fabric scrap

sew your buttons on securely!

Chunky, airy crochet isn't always the ideal base for sewing on a button. When sewing the button on this bag, I used an old tailoring trick. By placing a scrap of matching fabric or felt and a shirt button on the wrong side of the crochet behind the main button you can provide something for the sewing thread to grab on to. Just stitch through the shirt button, the fabric scrap, and the crochet each time your thread catches in the main button.

Sew button to center of front of bag 1¹⁄₄in/3cm from top edge. Attach both ends of cord to center top edge of back to correspond with button. If desired, line bag with fabric (see page 121). Trim off frayed fabric ends.

twine basket

Twine is a great choice for a sturdy shopper because it is very tough and holds its shape well. This basket starts with a circle and is worked with two strands of garden twine held together and a 12.00mm (US size O/P-15) hook. Cotton yarn and fabric strips provide the simple stripes. The basket gave me a platform to indulge my love of beads. Searching for just the right beads for the finished piece was nearly as enjoyable as the crocheting process. In the end I chose two alternative bead types, the ones in neutral shades (see left) dress the basket down a bit and the bright yellow ones (see right and top left) give it a snappier look. Take the twine and samples of the stripe accents with you when you choose your beads to get just the right color.

here's how...

The basket is worked round and round in a continuous spiral, so be sure to place the marker at the beginning of each round to keep track of where rounds begin and end (see the tip box opposite).

how big is it?
The finished basket measures approximately 10¼in/26cm in diameter x 12¼in/30.5cm tall.

which stitches?
Single crochet (sc)

how much "yarn"?
MC = twine in main color
   383yd/350m of natural garden twine
A = cotton fabric strips in first contrasting color
   ¼yd/20cm of 53in/135cm wide green cotton, or
   ½yd/30cm of 44in/112cm wide green cotton
B = medium-weight cotton yarn in second contrasting color
   1 x 1¾oz/50g ball Rowan *All Seasons Cotton* (turquoise—shade no. 185—or chosen color)
(*See page 124 for yarn tips*)

which hook?
12mm (US size O/P-15) crochet hook

or make this!

Twine and rags are perfect candidates for a rug. To make a rug, start out as for the basket, then after the eighth round carry on increasing twelve stitches on every alternate round until the rug is the desired size.

what gauge?
6 sts and 7½ rows to 4in/10cm measured over sc using two strands MC held tog and 12mm (US size O/P-15) hook.

any extras?
- 6 or 16 beads, ½in/12mm in diameter
- Sewing thread for stitching on beads

before you start
- Make a swatch of single crochet to check your gauge before beginning. If your twine is finer or thicker than the one used here, you may need to use more or fewer strands to get the right gauge. (See page 25 for more about gauge.)
- Cut (or tear) your fabric strips ¾–1in/2–2.5cm wide (see pages 97 and 117 for how to prepare fabric strips).
- To change to a new color, drop the color you are working with when there are two loops on the hook and complete the sc with the new color (see page 89).
- Work over the ends of the yarns to avoid having to weave them in later.
- *For crochet abbreviations, turn to page 127.*

make the foundation ring
Using a 12mm (US size O/P-15) hook and two strands MC held tog, ch4 and join with a sl st in first ch to form a ring.
1st rnd (RS) Ch1, 8sc in ring. (Do not turn at end of rnds, but work with RS always facing.)
Position marker as explained opposite.
2nd rnd 2sc in each sc. (16sc)
3rd rnd *1sc in next sc, 2sc in next sc; rep from * to end. (24sc)
4th rnd 1sc in each sc to end of rnd.

5th rnd *1sc in next sc, 2sc in next sc; rep from * to end. (36sc)

6th rnd As 4th rnd.

7th rnd *1sc in each of next 2sc, 2sc in next sc; rep from * to end. (48sc)

8th rnd As 4th rnd.

9th rnd As 4th rnd.

10th rnd Working into back lp of top of each sc, work 1sc in each sc to end.

(The last rnd forms a lip around base of basket, and rem rnds are worked without incs so that the basket grows upward.)

11th rnd Working into both lps of top of each sc in usual way, 1sc in each sc to end of rnd.

12th rnd As 11th rnd.

13th rnd As 11th rnd, but dropping MC inside basket and changing to A (fabric strip) with last yo of last sc.

14th rnd Using A, as 11th rnd, but dropping A and changing back to two strands MC with last yo of last sc.

Break off A.

Carrying MC up WS of crochet and breaking off B and A after each stripe, cont in sc in stripes as foll:

7 rnds, using two strands MC.

1 rnd, using three strands B.

3 rnds, using two strands MC.

1 rnd, using A (fabric strip).

2 rnds, using two strands MC.

Handles

Cont with two strands MC, start handles on next rnd as foll:

Next rnd 1sc in each of first 10sc, ch8, skip next 4sc, 1sc in each of next 20sc, ch8, skip next 4sc, 1sc in each of last 10sc.

Next rnd 1sc in each sc and each ch to end. (56sc)

Next 2 rnds 1sc in each sc to end.

Work 1 sl st in next sc and fasten off.

keep track of your rounds!

To keep track of where rounds start and finish, position a strand of contrasting yarn at the end of each round. To do this, before starting the next round, place the contrasting strand across the crochet fabric from front to back, close up against the loop on the hook and above the working yarn (see colored marker above). Start to work the first single crochet of the following round, catching the marker in position (see arrow above). The marker marks the start of the round and is caught under the top of the first stitch of the round. It is pulled out afterward.

finishing touches

Weave in any loose ends.

Stitch 16 beads around bag, or only three beads under each handle. Sew beads in place with sewing thread, positioning them just below last stripe in A and with 3sc between them.

net bags

Net bags are super-handy. Because they scrunch up into practically nothing, you can carry one around in your handbag and pull it out as the need arises. Here are three crochet versions of this practical bag, each with a different strap. They are made in one piece with rows of single crochet, but when worked on a huge hook and stretched out for use, this simple stitch is hard to recognize. Shown here, the Bag with Leather Handles is worked with a stylish tape yarn and the handles are added at the end (see page 85 for instructions). Twisted cords form the handles for the cotton Drawstring Bag on page 83. Embroidery hoops were used on the Bag with Wooden Handles on page 84.

here's how...

These bags look small as you crochet them, but they expand to hold quite a lot. The airy, open look of the crochet fabric only appears when you stretch it before joining the side seams.

how big is it?
Drawstring bag: The finished bag measures approximately 15in/38cm wide x 12in/30.5cm tall, excluding ruffle above drawstring.
Bag with wooden handles: The finished bag measures approximately 15in/38cm wide x 12in/30.5cm tall.
Bag with leather handles: The finished bag measures approximately 15in/38cm wide x 12in/30.5cm tall.

which stitches?
Single crochet (sc)

how much yarn?
Drawstring bag
MC = medium-weight cotton yarn in main color
   2 x 1¾oz/50g balls Rowan *All Seasons Cotton*
   (coral—shade no. 183—or chosen color)
CC = medium-weight cotton yarn in contrasting color
   small amount of Rowan *All Seasons Cotton*
   (gray—shade no. 170—or chosen color)
Bag with wooden handles
Cotton tape yarn
   3 x 1¾oz/50g balls Rowan *Cotton Tape*
   (purple—shade no. 550—or chosen color)
Bag with leather handles
Linen and cotton tape yarn
   3 x 1¾oz/50g balls Rowan *Linen Tape*
   (shade no. 347—or chosen color)
(*See page 124 for yarn tips*)

which hooks?
8.00mm and 15.00mm (US sizes L-11 and Q) crochet hooks

any extras?
- **Bag with wooden handles:** two wooden embroidery hoop frames 5in/12.5cm in diameter (or wooden ring handles from a craft shop), painted with acrylics in desired color; plus 16 beads with large eyes (eight each of two different bead types)
- **Bag with leather handles:** 11yd/10m leather string (2mm in diameter) in desired color

what gauge?
Approximately 8 sts and 8 rows to 4in/10cm measured over sc (unstretched) using 15.00mm (US size Q) hook.

before you start
- There is no need to check your gauge before beginning, as an exact size is not essential for a bag.
- Working the foundation chain for the bags loosely, as instructed, makes the first row easier.
- *For crochet abbreviations, turn to page 127.*

drawstring bag

make the foundation chain
The Drawstring Bag on the opposite page is worked in one long piece that is folded in half.
Using a 15.00mm (US size Q) hook and MC, ch31 loosely.
1st row 1sc in 2nd ch from hook, 1sc in each of rem 29ch. Turn. (30sc)

2nd row Ch1, 1sc in each sc to end. Turn.

Rep last row 36 times more (for a total of 38 rows worked from beg).

Do not fasten off MC.

finishing touches

Change to a 8.00mm (US size L-11) hook and cont with MC to work edging on next row of bag as foll:

Edging row (RS) Ch1, [1sc in next sc, 2sc in next sc] 15 times.

Fasten off.

Using a 8.00mm (US size L-11) hook and MC, work edging along other end (foundation-ch end) of bag with RS facing as foll:

Edging row (RS) Join on yarn with a sl st in hole above first foundation ch (between sts of first row), ch1, 1sc in same place as sl st, 2sc in next hole above next foundation ch, [1sc in next hole, 2sc in next hole] 14 times.

Fasten off.

Seams

To elongate sts, stretch crochet lengthwise before joining side seams. Then fold bag in half widthwise, with WS tog and lining up holes (between rows) along sides of crochet.

Using a 8.00mm (US size L-11) hook and MC and beg at bottom of one side seam, join on yarn with a sl st in first hole along edge (inserting hook through both layers), ch1, 2sc in same place as sl st, 2sc in each hole to top, working last sc through edging at top of bag.

Join other side seam in same way, but starting at top of bag.

Weave in any loose ends.

Drawstring cords

See tip box right for how to make two drawstrings for the bag.

drawstring cords

The drawstrings for the Drawstring Bag are two twisted cords. Each of the cords measures 48in/122cm long including the knotted ends. To make the cords, cut two 4yd/3.7m lengths of the contrasting color (CC) and one 4yd/3.7m length of the main color (MC). Make twisted cords from these lengths held together as explained on page 123. Thread the drawstrings through the bag below the third row from the top of the bag, with the ends of one drawstring at one side seam and the ends of the second drawstring at the other side seam. Knot the ends of each cord together.

Rep last row 34 times more (for a total of 36 rows worked from beg). Do not fasten off yarn.**

finishing touches

Change to a 8.00mm (US size L-11) hook and join crochet to first wooden hoop handle with sc as foll:
Joining row (RS) Hold hook with lp in front of wooden hoop handle and hold working yarn behind (and inside) hoop, then reach over hoop and ch1; next, insert hook through first sc of row (below hoop), reach under hoop, yo and draw a lp through, reach above hoop, yo and draw through 2 lps on hook to complete sc; cont in this way working 1sc in each sc to end (work sts close tog but not too tightly so sts can still slide along hoop).
Fasten off.
Join second hoop handle to other end (foundation-ch end) of bag in same way, but starting with a sl st in first foundation ch.

Seams

***To elongate sts, stretch crochet lengthwise before joining side seams. Then fold bag in half widthwise, with WS tog and lining up holes (between rows) along sides of crochet.
Using a 8.00mm (US size L-11) hook and beg at bottom of one side seam, join on yarn with a sl st in first hole along edge (inserting hook through both layers), ch1, 2sc in same place as sl st, 2sc in each hole to within last 6 holes from handle, 1sc in 6th hole from handle.
Fasten off.
Join other side seam in same way, but starting at 6th hole from handle and working toward bottom fold.
Weave in any loose ends.***

Attach beads

String four beads onto a 12in/30cm long strand of yarn, using two beads of each bead type. To hold on beads, make a knot at each end of strand so knots are 9in/23cm apart. Trim yarn ends close to knots. With two beads at each end of knotted strand, fold strand in half and loop onto an end st on handle

wooden handles

I bought two small embroidery hoops for the handles for the Bag with Wooden Handles above. These hoop frames come in a range of sizes, so, if you like, you can use bigger ones to change the look of the bag.

bag with wooden handles

make the foundation chain

The Bag with Wooden Handles shown above is worked in one long piece of single crochet that is folded in half.
**Using a 15.00mm (US size Q) hook, ch31 loosely.
1st row 1sc in 2nd ch from hook, 1sc in each of rem 29ch. Turn. (30sc)
2nd row Ch1, 1sc in each sc to end. Turn.

string the beads like this!

Even if your beads have big holes, it may not be that easy to pass crochet yarn through them. Here's a foolproof method. Fold a length of sewing thread in half and pass the two ends through a fine sewing needle. Then just loop the yarn through the loop of sewing thread and draw it through the beads one at a time as shown above.

(attach as you would fringe—see page122 for how to attach fringe). Make three more beaded strands and attach to three rem end sts on handles.

bag with leather handles

make the foundation chain
To work the Bag with Leather Handles on page 81, work as for Bag with Wooden Handles from ** to **.

finishing touches
Before joining last row of crochet to a handle, set aside and make handles as foll:

Leather handles
Cut a piece of cardboard 6½in/16.5cm wide. Then leaving a 5in/13cm length at beg, wrap leather string loosely five times around cardboard. Knot

short loose end to long loose end close to cardboard and slip wraps off cardboard, keeping rings tog. With long loose end and 8.00mm (US size L-11) hook, work 18sc loosely around leather rings, spacing sts apart. Do not fasten off, but set aside. Next, pick up crochet again, and using a 8.00mm (US size L-11) hook and yarn, join crochet to unworked section of leather handle with sc as foll:

Joining row (RS) Hold hook with lp in front of leather handle and hold working yarn behind (and inside) handle, then reach over handle and ch1; next, insert hook through first sc of row (below handle), reach under handle, yo and draw a lp through, reach above handle, yo and draw through 2 lps on hook to complete sc; cont in this way working 1sc in each sc to end (work sts close tog but not too tightly so sts can still slide along handle).
Fasten off.
If there is still any uncovered section on handle, cover with a few more leather sc, then fasten off leather. Thread leather ends inside yarn sc on handle. Secure each end of joining row to a leather sc with a few sts using yarn and yarn needle.
Make and join on a second handle to other end (foundation-ch end) of bag in same way, but starting with a sl st in first foundation ch.

Seams
Work seams as for Bag with Wooden Handles from *** to ***.

striped throw

Crochet is great for making throws from soft, cozy yarns. Unlike knitting, crochet can be worked across any width because only one stitch is worked at once. With knitting all the stitches have to fit onto a long circular needle, so there's a limit to the size of the piece. This generous-size, lightweight throw is made with chunky cotton chenille worked in double crochet and striped with a superchunky wool worked in single crochet. Amazingly, I made it, excluding the fringing, in about 12 hours. And I'm not a particularly speedy crocheter. The fringe softens the whole effect of the texture and, as with all finishing touches, it should be added with care to give your work the treasured heirloom look.

here's how...

You can use the stripe pattern given in these instructions or create your own stripe variation. Using the same two contrasting colors for the throw, you can make any number of stripe combinations, varying the thickness of the stripes. If the color is changed every two or four rows, there is no need to break off the yarn after every stripe—you can simply carry the yarn up the side of the throw.

how big is it?

The finished throw measures approximately 48³/₄in/122cm wide x 62in/157cm long.

which stitches?

- Single crochet (sc)
- Double crochet (dc)

how much yarn?

MC = chunky cotton chenille yarn in main color
9 x 3¹/₂oz/100g balls Rowan *Chunky Cotton*

try this!

- To avoid having to weave in lots of loose ends, when changing colors lay the loose ends of yarn over the top of the previous row and work your stitches over them.

- When working the chenille stripes in this throw, use two strands of it held together to create a thicker yarn. The best way to do this is to pull one strand out of the center of the ball and pair it with the strand starting on the outside of the ball.

Chenille (aqua blue—shade no. 392—or chosen color)
CC = superthick yarn in contrasting color
5 x 3¹/₂oz/100g balls Rowan *Big Wool*
(blue—shade no. 010—or chosen color)
(*See page 124 for yarn tips*)

which hook?

15.00mm (US size Q) crochet hook

what gauge?

- 6 sts to 4in/10cm measured over stripe patt using 15.00mm (US size Q) hook.
- 5 stripe patt rows (3 rows dc using two strands MC held tog and 2 rows sc using one strand CC) to 5¹/₂in/14cm using 15.00mm (US size Q) hook.

before you start

- There is no need to check your gauge before beginning, as an exact size is not essential for a throw.
- To create a chain edge along the foundation-chain edge of the throw, work the first row of sc into the back loop of each chain (see page 31).
- When making the throw, remember to always use two strands of the chenille yarn (MC) held together, but use only one strand of the superthick wool yarn (CC).
- *For crochet abbreviations, turn to page 127.*

make the foundation chain

Using a 15.00mm (US size Q) hook and CC, ch74. Beg stripe patt as foll:
1st row Using CC, 1sc in 2nd ch from hook, 1sc in each of rem 72ch. Turn. (73sc)
2nd row Using CC, ch1, 1sc in each sc to end, changing to two strands MC with last yo of last sc of

row (see right for how to change colors). Turn.
Break off CC.

Cont patt using two strands MC and one strand CC throughout as foll:

3rd row Using MC, ch3 (to count as first dc), skip first sc, *1dc in next sc; rep from * to end. Turn. (73 sts)

4th row Using MC, ch3, skip first dc, *1dc in next dc; rep from *, ending with 1dc in 3rd of ch3. Turn.

5th row As 4th row, but changing to CC with last yo of last dc of row. Turn.
Break off MC.

6th row Using CC, ch1, 1sc in each dc to end, ending with 1sc in 3rd of ch3. Turn.

7th row Using CC, ch1, 1sc in each sc to end, changing to MC with last yo of last sc of row. Turn.
Break off CC.

Rep 3rd–7th rows to form stripe patt and cont in stripe patt until throw measures approximately 62in/157cm long, ending with 2 CC rows.
Fasten off.

finishing touches

Weave in any loose ends.

Side edging

Using a 15.00mm (US size Q) hook and CC, work a row of sc along two sides of throw from top of last row to foundation-ch edge. To work this edging, work 4sc evenly along row-ends of each MC stripe and 2sc along row-ends of each CC stripe.

Fringe

Attach 25 groups of fringe evenly along top and bottom of throw (foundation-ch edge and last-row edge). For each group of fringe, use eight strands of MC, each 16in/40cm long. Fold each group of eight strands in half and pull through edge of throw (see page 122). To attach fringe groups evenly,

change colors like this!

When changing colors in your crochet it is usually best to do so when completing the last loop of the previous stitch. This is so that the loop on the hook after you have completed the stitch is in the new color and will match the color used for the next stitch. Whether changing colors at the end of a row or in the middle of the row (as shown above), complete whatever stitch you are working up to the last loop needed, then draw through the new color to finish the stitch. The illustration above shows a completed single crochet with the new color on the hook ready to start the next stitch. The same principle applies for half double crochet or double crochet.

position one group in first and last st of foundation ch, and one group in every 3rd st of foundation ch in between.

patterned throws

Made with simple pattern stitches, these two throws will give you a taste of how basic crochet stitches can be combined to make smart multicolored textures. The Brick-stitch Throw on the left uses three colors and is edged with one row of simple double crochet. Made with a hook 15 millimeters in diameter (US size Q) and superthick wool yarns, the giant loops have a surprisingly contemporary look. The black-and-white Bicolor Throw shown right and on page 93 is just as quick and easy—you can make it in any two colors you like. After working only a few rows of either throw, you'll be able to continue without even reading the pattern again.

here's how...

The Brick-stitch Throw shown on page 90 has written row-by-row instructions. For the row-by-row instructions for the Bicolor Throw (see detail opposite), follow the simple symbol chart provided.

how big is it?
Brick-stitch throw: The finished throw measures approximately 52in/130cm wide x 67in/168cm long.
Bicolor throw: The finished throw measures approximately 48³⁄₄in/122cm wide x 58¹⁄₂in/149cm long.

which stitches?
- Double crochet (dc), for Brick-stitch Throw
- Double crochet (dc) and single crochet (sc), for Bicolor Throw

how much yarn?
Brick-stitch throw

A = superchunky wool yarn in first contrasting color
  6 x 3¹⁄₂oz/100g balls Rowan *Big Wool*
  (black—shade no. 008—or chosen color)
B = superchunky wool yarn in second contrasting color
  7 x 3¹⁄₂oz/100g balls Rowan *Big Wool*
  (grape—shade no. 025—or chosen color)
C = superchunky wool yarn in third contrasting color
  6 x 3¹⁄₂oz/100g balls Rowan *Big Wool*
  (white—shade no. 001—or chosen color)

Bicolor throw

MC = superchunky wool yarn in main color
  9 x 3¹⁄₂oz/100g balls Rowan *Big Wool*
  (white—shade no. 001—or chosen color)
CC = superchunky wool yarn in contrasting color
  8 x 3¹⁄₂oz/100g balls Rowan *Big Wool*
  (black—shade no. 008—or chosen color)
(*See page 124 for yarn tips*)

which hooks?
12.00mm and 15.00mm (US sizes O/P-15 and Q) crochet hooks

what gauge?
Brick-stitch throw: Approximately 6¹⁄₂ sts and 5 rows to 4in/10cm measured over brick-stitch patt using 15.00mm (US size Q) hook.
Bicolor throw: 6 sts and 5 rows to 4in/10cm measured over bicolor patt using 15.00mm (US size Q) hook.

before you start
- There is no need to check your gauge before beginning, as an exact size is not essential for a throw.
- *For crochet abbreviations, turn to page 127.*

brick-stitch throw

make the foundation chain
Using a 15.00mm (US size Q) hook and A, ch84.
1st patt row 1dc in 4th ch from hook, 1dc in each of next 3ch, ch4, skip next 4ch, *1dc in each of next 4ch, ch4, skip next 4ch; rep from *, ending with 1dc in last ch. Turn. (82 sts, counting each ch, each dc, and ch3 at beg of row as one st)
Drop A at side of work, but do not break off.
2nd patt row Using B, ch3, 1dc in each of first 4ch skipped in last row (working around ch4 above), ch4, skip next 4dc, *1dc in each of next 4ch skipped in last row, ch4, skip next 4dc; rep from *, ending with 1sc in 3rd of ch3. Turn.
Drop B at side of work, but do not break off.
3rd patt row Using C, ch3, 1dc in each of first 4dc skipped in last row, ch4, skip next 4dc, *1dc in each

of next 4dc skipped in last row, ch4, skip next 4dc; rep from *, ending with 1sc in 3rd of ch3. Turn. Drop C at side of work, but do not break off.

4th patt row Using A, as 3rd patt row.

Drop A at side of work, but do not break off.

5th patt row Using B, as 3rd patt row.

Drop B at side of work, but do not break off.

Rep 3rd–5th patt rows to form patt and cont in patt until throw measures 65½in/164cm from foundation-ch edge, ending with a 3rd patt row. Break off B and C and work last row as foll:

Last row Using A, ch2, 1dc in each of first 4dc skipped in last row, 1sc in each of next 4dc, *1dc in each of next 4dc skipped in last row, 1sc in each of next 4dc; rep from *, ending with 1sc in 3rd of ch3. Fasten off.

finishing touches

Using a 12.00mm hook (US size O/P-15) and B, work dc edging around throw as foll:

Edging rnd Starting along foundation-ch edge, join B with a sl st to corner ch of foundation, ch3 to count as first dc, 2dc in same place as sl st, 1dc in each ch to last ch, 3dc in last ch; work dc evenly along side edge; 3dc in first st along top of throw, 1dc in each st to last st, 3dc in last st; work dc evenly along second side edge; join with a sl st to 3rd of ch3 at beg of rnd.

Fasten off.

Weave in any loose ends.

bicolor throw

Using a 15.00mm (US size Q) hook and MC, ch72. Foll symbol chart below (see page 17 for symbol key) for patt, using MC for first and 3rd rows and CC for 2nd row. Work first row (71sc), then extend loop on hook, remove hook and return to beg of row just worked to work 2nd row in CC (starting with a sl st). At beg of 3rd row, pull extended MC loop through CC loop, then work 3rd row in MC. (Work dc in 3rd row into skipped sc in row below and around ch.)

Rep 2nd and 3rd rows to form patt, until throw measures 57in/145cm. Fasten off. Finish as for Brick-stitch Throw, using MC for edging.

circle rag rug

The circular shape of this huge-hook rug is formed by working single crochet round and round in a spiral. The color scheme and stripe sequence is just a suggestion. Choose five colors that harmonize nicely and that suit your décor. A bicolor rug would also be effective—perhaps with a dark solid ground and a single-row stripe on every fifth row. With the exception of fabrics that are too thick or too stiff, most materials are fine for "rag" crochet. The cotton fabrics used for the "yarn" on this rug give the crochet body, and the felt strips add a lovely contrasting texture.

here's how...

There is no need to exactly match the specified stitch size for this rug (see What Gauge?). In fact, the crochet circle pattern works for any stitch size, and you can keep working the rug round and round until it is the desired size.

how big is it?
The finished rug measures approximately 36¼in/91cm in diameter, but the size is adjustable.

which stitches?
Single crochet (sc)

how much "yarn"?
A = cotton fabric strips in first contrasting color
    2yd/1.8m of 44in/112cm wide lavender cotton

B = felt strips in second contrasting color
    1¾yd/1.5m of 37in/94cm wide gold felt

C = cotton fabric strips in third contrasting color
    2½yd/2.2m of 44in/112cm wide blue cotton

D = fabric strips in fourth contrasting color
    2yd/1.8m of 44in/112cm wide gold and coral polka dot fabric

E = cotton fabric strips in fifth contrasting color
    2¼yd/2m of 44in/112cm wide turquoise cotton

which hook?
15.00mm (US size Q) crochet hook

what gauge?
Approximately 5½ sts and 5½ rows to 4in/10cm measured over sc using 15.00mm (US size Q) hook.

fabrics for "rag" crochet
A range of fabric types was used for the Circles Rag Rug, including lightweight pure cotton in three shades, gold cotton felt, and a synthetic polka dot that drapes. The cotton fabrics give the rug strength and body, so be sure to include these in your design if you are making up your own. You could also wrap each strip of fabric around string as you work; this would add extra strength and extra weight, for a very durable rug.

before you start

- Cut the felt strips 1/2in/12mm wide or just slightly under this width (see right and page 117 for tips on cutting). The felt can be more stretchy either across the width or lengthwise, so cut the strips in the direction that is less stretchy. Cut or tear the cotton-fabric strips about 1–1 1/2in/2.5–4cm wide depending on the fabric thickness—wider for fine cotton and narrower for medium-weight cotton. Make a small swatch of single crochet to test the strip width if you are unsure.
- To keep track of where rounds start and finish, position a strand of contrasting yarn at the end of each round. To do this, before starting the next round, place the contrasting strand across the crochet fabric from front to back, close up against the loop on the hook and *above the working yarn*. Start to work the first sc of the following round, catching the marker in position. The marker marks the start of the round and is caught under the top of the first stitch of the round. (See page 79 for an illustration of this marking technique.)
- To change to a new color, drop the color you are working with when there are two loops on the hook and complete the sc with the new color (see page 89).
- Work over the ends of the fabric strips to avoid having to weave them in later.
- *For crochet abbreviations, turn to page 127.*

make the foundation ring

Using a 15.00mm (US size Q) hook and A, ch4 and join with a sl st in first ch to form a ring.

1st rnd (RS) Ch1, 8sc in ring. (Do not turn at end of rnds, but work with RS always facing.)

Position marker as explained in Before You Start.

2nd rnd 2sc in each sc. (16sc)

A

B

rag strips in a jiffy!

I usually tear my continuous "rag" strips for crochet, but some fabrics won't cooperate. Felt, for instance, can be torn but not in neat, even strips. If you are only cutting a few strips, you can cut back and forth as shown on page 117, but if you need to cut masses of strips, such as for a rug, try this quick technique. Fold your fabric in half lengthwise, aligning the selvages. Then fold the fabric again lengthwise, positioning the first fold about 2in/5cm from the selvages. Starting at the second fold, cut the first strip from the fold toward the selvages, cutting through the first fold and ending the cut about 3/8in/1cm from the selvages. Continue cutting strips in this way, leaving them all joined at the top (A). To create the continuous strip, clip through the bottom layer of fabric at the top of the first strip. When you unravel the first strip, you'll see where to clip through the fabric at the selvage to create the continuous strip (B).

Changing colors as desired (see Before You Start and illustration on page 89) and using B (felt) for at least every third or fourth row throughout, cont working rnds to shape rug as foll:

3rd rnd *1sc in next sc, 2sc in next sc; rep from *. (24sc)

4th rnd 1sc in each sc.

5th rnd *1sc in next sc, 2sc in next sc; rep from *. (36sc)

6th rnd As 4th rnd.

7th rnd *1sc in each of next 2sc, 2sc in next sc; rep from *. (48sc)

8th rnd As 4th rnd.

9th rnd *1sc in each of next 3sc, 2sc in next sc; rep from *. (60sc)

10th rnd As 4th rnd.

11th rnd 1sc in each of first 2sc, 2sc in next sc, *1sc in each of next 4sc, 2sc in next sc; rep from *, ending with 1sc in each of last 2sc. (72sc)

12th rnd As 4th rnd.

13th rnd *1sc in each of next 5sc, 2sc in next sc; rep from *. (84sc)

14th rnd As 4th rnd.

15th rnd 1sc in each of first 3sc, 2sc in next sc, *1sc in each of next 6sc, 2sc in next sc; rep from *, ending with 1sc in each of last 3sc. (96sc)

16th rnd As 4th rnd.

17th rnd *1sc in each of next 7sc, 2sc in next sc; rep from *. (108sc)

18th rnd As 4th rnd.

19th rnd 1sc in each of first 4sc, 2sc in next sc, *1sc in each of next 8sc, 2sc in next sc; rep from *, ending with 1sc in each of last 4sc. (120sc)

20th rnd As 4th rnd.

21st rnd *1sc in each of next 9sc, 2sc in next sc; rep from *. (132sc)

22nd rnd As 4th rnd.

23rd rnd 1sc in each of first 5sc, 2sc in next sc, *1sc in each of next 10sc, 2sc in next sc; rep from *, ending with 1sc in each of last 5sc. (144sc)

24th rnd As 4th rnd.

25th rnd *1sc in each of next 11sc, 2sc in next sc; rep from *. (156sc)

(If desired cont in this way, adding 12 extra sc in every alternate rnd until rug is desired size.)

Work 1 sl st in next sc and fasten off.

finishing touches

Weave in any loose ends of fabric strips into stitches on WS of rug.

or make this!

- This circle pattern can be used for many other things, using the same "rag" fabrics. For a cushion cover, work two circles of the desired size. With wrong sides facing and using double-sided backstitch (see page 120) for an outside seam, stitch the circles together leaving an opening for inserting the pillow-form/cushion pad. Then insert the pillow-form/cushion pad and stitch the opening closed.

- You could also use the pattern to make a circular bag. Make two pieces to the size you want, then sew them together as for the cushion suggestion, and add a strap.

square medallion cushion

This variegated yarn is just sensational. Its vibrant colors and the thin and thick texture are really eyecatching. To show it off to the full, I have crocheted it into a simple square medallion shape to make a cushion. Worked from the center outward, the medallion is a traditional crochet square. Since it is worked in the round, you can make it to any size with no trouble at all. Two smaller pieces stitched together, with the addition of a strap, would make a great little bag.

here's how...

You can keep adding rounds to this cushion until it is the right size, so there is no need to worry about obtaining an exact stitch size—the gauge is given just as a rough guide (see right).

how big is it?
The finished cushion measures 17in/43cm square.

which stitches?
Single crochet (sc)

how much yarn?
A = variegated chunky wool yarn in first contrasting color
1 x 3¹/₂oz/100g ball Colinette *Point 5* (dusty violet—shade no. 100—or chosen color)
B = variegated chunky wool yarn in second contrasting color
1 x 3¹/₂oz/100g ball Colinette *Point 5* (hot pink—shade no. 134—or chosen color)
C = variegated chunky wool yarn in third contrasting color
1 x 3¹/₂oz/100g ball Colinette *Point 5* (bright turquoise and blue—shade no. 18—or chosen color)
(*See page 124 for yarn tips*)

which hook?
12.00mm (US size O/P-15) crochet hook

try this!
When changing colors, work over ends of yarn to avoid having to weave in ends later.

what gauge?
6 sts and 6 rows to 4in/10cm measured over sc using 12.00mm (US size O/P-15) hook.

any extras?
- A complementary dark cotton fabric and matching sewing thread for cushion cover—one piece 18in/46cm square for the front, and two pieces each 18in/46cm by 12in/31cm for the overlapping backs
- Pillow-form/cushion pad to fit

before you start
- When working the first round, wrap the tail end of the yarn clockwise around the ring and work your 12 single crochet stitches over it. Then later you can pull the tail end to tighten up the hole at the center.
- In order not to confuse the slip stitch worked to join the rounds with a single crochet stitch, be sure to count the stitches between the corners as you are working them. Count your stitches at the end of the first few rounds just to make sure.
- *For crochet abbreviations, turn to page 127.*

make the foundation ring
The crochet is for the front of the cushion only and is stitched to the front of a fabric cushion cover. Using a 12.00mm (US size O/P-15) hook and A, ch4 and join with a sl st in first ch to form a ring. Beg stripe patt as foll:

1st rnd (RS) Using A, ch1, 12sc in ring, join with a sl st in first sc. (Do not turn at end of rnds, but work with RS always facing.)
2nd rnd Using A, ch1, 2sc in same place as sl st, [1sc in each of next 2sc, 3sc in next sc] 3 times, 1sc in each of next 2sc, 1sc in same place as first 2sc-group

of rnd were worked, join with a sl st in first sc of 2sc-group. (20sc)

3rd rnd Using A, ch1, 2sc in same place as sl st, [1sc in each of next 4sc, 3sc in next sc] 3 times, 1sc in each of next 4sc, 1sc in same place as first 2sc-group of round were worked, break off A and using B join with a sl st in first sc of 2sc-group. (28sc)

4th rnd Using B, ch1, 2sc in same place as sl st, [1sc in each of next 6sc, 3sc in next sc] 3 times, 1sc in each of next 6sc, 1sc in same place as first 2sc-group of rnd were worked, join with a sl st in first sc of 2sc-group. (36sc)

5th rnd Using B, ch1, 2sc in same place as sl st, [1sc in each of next 8sc, 3sc in next sc] 3 times, 1sc in each of next 8sc, 1sc in same place as first 2sc-group of rnd were worked, join with a sl st in first sc of 2sc-group. (44sc)

6th rnd Using B, ch1, 2sc in same place as sl st, [1sc in each of next 10sc, 3sc in next sc] 3 times, 1sc in each of next 10sc, 1sc in same place as first 2sc-group of rnd were worked, break off B and using A join with a sl st in first sc of 2sc-group. (52sc)

7th rnd Using A, ch1, 2sc in same place as sl st, [1sc in each of next 12sc, 3sc in next sc] 3 times, 1sc in each of next 12sc, 1sc in same place as first 2sc-group of rnd were worked, join with a sl st in first sc of 2sc-group. (60sc)

8th rnd Using A, ch1, 2sc in same place as sl st was worked, [1sc in each of next 14sc, 3sc in next sc] 3 times, 1sc in each of next 14sc, 1sc in same place as first 2sc-group of rnd were worked, join with a sl st in first sc of 2sc-group. (68sc)

9th rnd Using A, ch1, 2sc in same place as sl st, [1sc in each of next 16sc, 3sc in next sc] 3 times, 1sc in each of next 16sc, 1sc in same place as first 2sc-group of round were worked, break off A and using C join with a sl st in first sc of 2sc-group. (76sc)

10th rnd Using C, ch1, 2sc in same place as sl st, [1sc in each of next 18sc, 3sc in next sc] 3 times, 1sc in each of next 18sc, 1sc in same place as first 2sc-group of rnd were worked, join with a sl st in first sc of 2sc-group. (84sc)

11th rnd Using C, ch1, 2sc in same place as sl st, [1sc in each of next 20sc, 3sc in next sc] 3 times, 1sc in each of next 20sc, 1sc in same place as first 2sc-group of round were worked, break off C and using B join with a sl st in first sc of 2sc-group. (92sc)

12th rnd Using B, ch1, 2sc in same place as sl st, [1sc in each of next 22sc, 3sc in next sc] 3 times, 1sc in each of next 22sc, 1sc in same place as first 2sc-group of rnd were worked, join with a sl st in first sc of 2sc-group. (100sc)

13th rnd Using B, ch1, 2sc in same place as sl st, [1sc in each of next 24sc, 3sc in next sc] 3 times, 1sc in each of next 24sc, 1sc in same place as first 2sc-group of round were worked, break off B and using A join with a sl st in first sc of 2sc-group. (108sc)

14th rnd Using A, ch1, 1 sl st in each sc, join with a sl st in first sl st of rnd. Fasten off.

finishing touches

Weave in any loose ends on WS. Pin crochet out to correct size RS down on a padded surface. Gently press on WS using a damp cloth and a warm iron. To make fabric cover, pin one back piece to each side of front and sew seams with a 1/2in/1.5cm seam allowance. Turn under and stitch 1/2in/1.5cm hems along outer edges of backs (edges that will be along opening). Then fold backs onto front with RS tog and stitch remaining seams, leaving overlapping edges open. Turn RS out and press.
Using sewing thread, stitch crochet to front of fabric cover so that edges meet seamlines and hide them. Insert pillow-form/cushion-pad.

graphic cushions

Worked with three strands of medium-weight cotton yarn held together, the simple traditional crochet stitch pattern used for these three cushions creates a chunky, durable texture. The Big Circles Cushion (in the foreground right) and the Ribbon-tie Cushion (in the background) are crocheted all in white. The decorative circles are crocheted separately and stitched on later. The Button Cushion, shown on page 2 (in the background) and page 109, is plain white with an integrated black button border at one end. The fastenings on all the cushions provide touches of bright contrasting color.

here's how...

The stitch pattern on the cushions is formed with alternating chain-spaces and single crochet. The single crochet stitches are worked into the chain-spaces of the row below and the chain stitches are worked above the single crochet stitches.

how big is it?
Big circles cushion: The finished cover measures approximately 17³/₄in/45cm x 19³/₄in/50cm.
Ribbon-tie cushion: The finished cover measures approximately 13³/₄in/35cm x 19³/₄in/50cm.
Button cushion: The finished cover measures approximately 13³/₄in/35cm x 15³/₄in/40cm.

which stitches?
- Single crochet (sc)
- Chain spaces (ch-sp)

how much yarn?
Big circles cushion
MC = medium-weight cotton yarn in main color
  12 x 1³/₄oz/50g balls Rowan *All Seasons Cotton* (off-white—shade no. 178—or chosen color)
CC = chunky cotton chenille in contrasting color
  small amount of Rowan *Chunky Cotton Chenille* (black—shade no. 367—or chosen color)
A = medium-weight cotton yarn
  small amount of Rowan *All Seasons Cotton* (coral—shade no. 183—or chosen color)
B = lightweight silk and cotton blend yarn
  small amount of Rowan *Summer Tweed* (raspberry—shade no. 528—or chosen color)
Ribbon-tie cushion
MC = medium-weight cotton yarn in main color
  10 x 1³/₄oz/50g balls Rowan *All Seasons Cotton* (off-white—shade no. 178—or chosen color)
CC = chunky cotton chenille in contrasting color

small amount of Rowan *Chunky Cotton Chenille* (black—shade no. 367—or chosen color)
Button cushion
MC = medium-weight cotton yarn in main color
  7 x 1³/₄oz/50g balls Rowan *All Seasons Cotton* (off-white—shade no. 178—or chosen color)
CC = chunky cotton chenille in contrasting color
  1 x 3¹/₂oz/100g ball Rowan *Chunky Cotton Chenille* (black—shade no. 367—or chosen color)
(*See page 124 for yarn tips*)

which hook?
10.00mm (US size N-13) crochet hook

what gauge?
9 sts and 9 rows to 4in/10cm measured over patt st using three strands MC held tog and 10.00mm (US size N-13) hook.

any extras?
Big circles cushion: 17³/₄in/45cm square pillow-form/cushion pad
Ribbon-tie cushion: 13³/₄in/35cm x 17³/₄in/45cm pillow-form/cushion pad and 39in/99cm ribbon, ³/₄in/2cm wide
Button cushion: 13³/₄in/35cm square pillow-form/cushion pad and three buttons each 1³/₈in/3.5cm in diameter

before you start
- To work "into a ch-sp," insert the hook through the space under the chain (not into the chain itself).
- There is no need to check your gauge before beginning, as an exact size is not essential for a cushion. But wait until the cushion is complete before buying the pillow-form/cushion pad.

- The cushions are worked in the round, but you do not need to keep track of where the rounds beg and end. After the 3rd round has been completed, just work round and round until the cushion is the desired length.
- When one ball of yarn runs out, tie the strand from the new ball onto the end of the old ball. When you reach the knotted ends lay them over the top of the row below and work your stitches over them to hide them.
- *For crochet abbreviations, turn to page 127.*

For crochet abbreviations, turn to page 127.

big circles cushion

make the foundation ring

The Big Circles Cushion shown in the foreground on pages 104–105 is made in one piece.

Using a 10.00mm (US size N-13) hook and three strands MC held tog, ch81 and join with a sl st in first ch to form a ring.

Using three strands MC held tog, beg patt as foll:

1st rnd (RS) Ch1, 1sc in same place as sl st, *1sc in each of rem 80ch. (Do not turn at end of rnds, but work with RS always facing.)

2nd rnd 1sc in first sc of previous rnd, *ch1, skip next sc, 1sc in next sc; rep from * to end. (81 sts, counting each sc and each ch1 as one st)

3rd rnd Ch1, *1sc in next ch1-sp, ch1; rep from * to end.

Rep [1sc in next ch1-sp, ch1] until crochet measures 19¼in/49cm from foundation-ch edge, ending in line with tail end of yarn at beg of crochet (this marks one side-fold on cushion cover).

Work last rnd as foll:

Last rnd Work 1sc in each ch1-sp and 1sc in each sc to end, join with a sl st to first sc of rnd. Fasten off.

twisted cord fastening

Make a 29in/74cm long twisted cord for closing the Big Circles Cushion. Cut two 73in/185cm lengths each of A and B. With these four strands held together, make a cord as explained on page 123. Weave the cord in and out of both layers of the cushion cover 2in/5cm from the edges, and knot at each end.

finishing touches

Turn tube of crochet WS out. Pin two layers tog along foundation-ch edge, aligning tail end of yarn with a side-fold. Using one strand MC, join seam. Weave in any loose ends, then turn RS out.

Big circle motifs (make 4 alike)

Using a 10.00mm (US size N-13) hook and one strand CC and leaving a long loose end, ch15 and join with a sl st in first ch to form a ring.

1st rnd (RS) Ch3, 35dc in ring, join with a sl st in 3rd of ch3. Fasten off, leaving a long loose end. Distribute dc evenly around foundation ring.

Pin finished motifs, RS up, to cushion cover in desired positions. Using long loose ends, stitch in place around inner and outer edges.

Insert pillow-form/cushion pad. Make a cord to close as explained above.

ribbon-tie cushion

make the foundation ring

The Ribbon-tie Cushion shown below and in the background on page 105 is made in one piece. Using a 10.00mm (US size N-13) hook and three strands MC held tog, ch63 and join with a sl st in first ch to form a ring.

tie fastening

Adding ribbon ties is a really easy way to fasten the opening on a huge-hook crochet cushion cover. Push the ties through both layers of the crochet, about 2in/5cm from the edge, and tie or knot them together. Make sure you get a really wonderful ribbon for this important detail.

Using three strands MC held tog, beg patt as foll:

1st rnd (RS) Ch1, 1sc in same place as sl st, *1sc in each of rem 62ch. (Do not turn at end of rnds, but work with RS always facing.)

2nd rnd 1sc in first sc of previous rnd, *ch1, skip next sc, 1sc in next sc; rep from * to end. (63 sts, counting each sc and each ch1 as one st)

3rd rnd Ch1, *1sc in next ch1-sp, ch1; rep from * to end.

Rep [1sc in next ch1-sp, ch1] until crochet measures 19¼in/49cm from foundation-ch edge, ending in line with tail end of yarn at beg of crochet (this marks one side-fold on cushion cover).

Work last rnd as foll:

Last rnd Work 1sc in each ch1-sp and 1sc in each sc to end, join with a sl st to first sc of rnd. Fasten off.

finishing touches

Turn tube of crochet WS out. Pin two layers tog along foundation-ch edge, aligning the tail end of yarn with a side-fold. Using one strand MC, join seam. Weave in any loose ends, then turn RS out.

Little circle motifs (make 3 alike)

Make each circle for appliqué as foll:

Using a 10.00mm (US size N-13) hook and one strand CC and leaving a long loose end, ch3 and join with a sl st to first ch to form a ring.

1st rnd (RS) Ch3, then wind loose end of yarn around back of ring once and, working over it, work 12dc in ring, join with a sl st in 3rd of ch3. Fasten off, leaving a long loose end.

Pull loose end at center of ring to close hole, then thread end into a yarn needle and secure with a few sts on WS.

Pin finished motifs, RS up, on cushion cover in desired positions. Using long loose end and stitching around outer edges, secure circles in place.

Ribbon ties

Cut three ribbons, each 13in/33cm long and hem the ends to desired length. Insert pillow-form/cushion pad and tie on ribbons as explained left.

button cushion

make the foundation ring

The Button Cushion shown right (and in the background on page 2) is made in one piece. Using a 10.00mm (US size N-13) hook and three strands MC held tog, ch63 and join with a sl st in first ch to form a ring.

Using three strands MC held tog, beg patt as foll:

1st rnd (RS) Ch1, 1sc in same place as sl st, *1sc in each of rem 62ch. (Do not turn at end of rnds but work with RS always facing.)

2nd rnd 1sc in first sc of previous rnd, *ch1, skip next sc, 1sc in next sc; rep from * to end. (63 sts, counting each sc and each ch1 as one st)

3rd rnd Ch1, *1sc in next ch1-sp, ch1; rep from * to end.

Rep [1sc in next ch1-sp, ch1] until crochet measures 13³⁄₄in/35cm from foundation-ch edge, ending in line with tail end of yarn at beg of crochet (this marks one side-fold on cushion cover).

Break off MC. Using two strands CC, work 2 rnds more in patt, ending with ch1. (Be sure to end in line with side-fold.)

Still using two strands CC, work buttonholes as foll:

1st buttonhole rnd 1sc in next ch1-sp, [ch1, 1sc in next ch1-sp] twice, [ch3, skip next ch1-sp, 1sc in next ch1-sp, (ch1, 1sc in next ch1-sp) twice] 2 times, ch3, skip next ch1-sp, *1sc in next ch1-sp, ch1; rep from *, ending with 1sc in last ch1-sp.

2nd buttonhole rnd Work in patt, but when each ch3-sp is reached work [1sc, ch1, 1sc] all in ch3-sp. Work one rnd more in patt.

Work last rnd as foll:

Last rnd Work 1sc in each ch1-sp and 1sc in each sc to end, join with a sl st to first sc of rnd. Fasten off.

finishing touches

Turn tube of crochet WS out. Pin two layers tog along foundation-ch edge, aligning the tail end of yarn with a side-fold. Using one strand MC, join seam.

button fastening

There are only three buttons on the plain white Button Cushion (see page 2), so I splurged on these smart retro ones from a button store. If you have some special big buttons, base your cushion color scheme around them.

Weave in any loose ends, then turn RS out. If buttonholes are too big for your buttons, stitch tog at each end of each buttonhole to tighten. Sew buttons in place to correspond with buttonholes. Insert pillow-form/cushion pad and button to close.

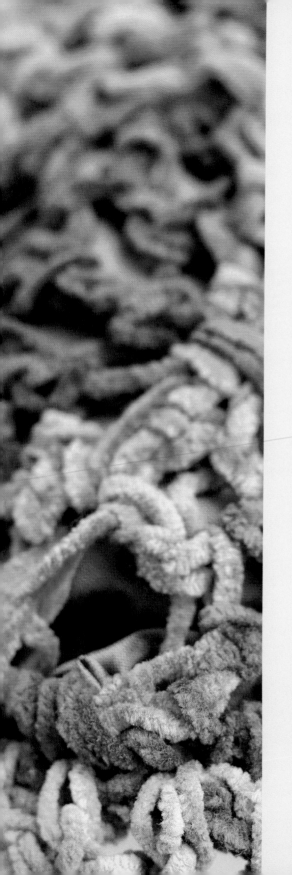

diamonds cushion

This cushion relies on a wonderfully textured stitch and soft chenille yarn for its appeal. The simple bicolor stitch pattern forms rows of staggered diamonds and is just one of hundreds of multicolored crochet patterns that you can find in crochet stitch pattern books. A little more complex than rows of simple single or double crochet stitches, when used for a basic rectangular shape it is well within the reach of a beginner. Worked here with a hook 10 millimeters in diameter (US size N-13) and a thick, soft cotton chenille yarn, the cover is lined with a toning fabric.

here's how...

Using just one strand of chunky cotton chenille for this stitch pattern creates an airy, see-through texture. For a more solid texture, you could use a thicker wool yarn with the same hook size; if you do this, aim for the same gauge (see right).

how big is it?
The finished cushion measures approximately 18in/45cm square.

which stitches?
- Single crochet (sc)
- Half double crochet (hdc)
- Double crochet (dc)
- Treble crochet (tr)

how much yarn?
A = chunky cotton chenille yarn in first contrasting color
   1 x 3¹/₂oz/100g ball Rowan *Chunky Cotton Chenille* (dark olive—shade no. 390—or chosen color)
B = chunky cotton chenille yarn in second contrasting color
   1 x 3¹/₂oz/100g ball Rowan *Chunky Cotton Chenille* (aqua blue—shade no. 392—or chosen color)

try this!

A beginner should practice the stitch first— see Before You Start for how many foundation chain to start with. It is best to use a chunky wool yarn for the practice swatch because it is easier to see stitches worked in wool. Then use the chenille for the gauge swatch.

C = chunky cotton chenille yarn in third contrasting color
   small amount of Rowan *Chunky Cotton Chenille* (light sage green—shade no. 393—or chosen color)
(*See page 124 for yarn tips*)

which hook?
10.00mm (US size N-13) crochet hook

what gauge?
7 sts and 6 rows to 4in/10cm measured over diamond patt using 10.00mm (US size N-13) hook.

any extras?
- A complementary dark olive fabric and matching sewing thread for a fabric cushion cover—one piece 19in/48cm square for the front, and two pieces each 19in/48cm by 12in/31cm for the overlapping back pieces
- Pillow-form/cushion pad to fit

before you start
- To check gauge, ch20 and repeat 1st–6th pattern rows until sample measures 5in/13cm.
- *For crochet abbreviations, turn to page 127.*

make the foundation chain
The cushion is made in two pieces—a front and a back.
Front and back (both alike)
Using a 10.00mm (US size N-13) hook and A, ch32.
1st patt row 1sc in 2nd ch from hook, *1hdc in next ch, 1dc in next ch, 1tr in next ch, 1dc in next ch, 1hdc in next ch, 1sc in next ch; rep from * to end, changing to B with last yo of last sc. Turn. (31 sts) Drop A at side of work, but do not break off.

2nd patt row Using B, ch3, skip first sc, *1dc in next st, 1hdc in next st, ch1, skip next st (tr), 1hdc in next st, 1dc in next st, 1tr in next st; rep from * to end. Turn. (31 sts, counting first ch3 as first st)

3rd patt row Using B, ch3, skip first tr, *1dc in next st, 1hdc in next st, 1sc in top of tr skipped in last row (working around ch1 worked in last row), 1hdc in next st, 1dc in next st, 1tr in next st, rep from *, working last tr in 3rd of ch3 and changing to A with last yo of this last tr (don't pull A too tightly when picking it up from end of row 2 rows below). Turn. Drop B at side of work, but do not break off.

4th patt row Using A, ch1, 1sc in first st, *1hdc in next st, 1dc in next st, 1tr in top of tr 2 rows below (in same place as sc in last row), 1dc in next st, 1hdc in next st, ch1, skip next st (tr), rep from *, omitting ch1 at end of last rep and working 1sc in 3rd of ch3. Turn.

5th patt row Using A, ch1, 1sc in first st, *1hdc in next st, 1dc in next st, 1tr in next st, 1dc in next st, 1hdc in next st, 1sc in top of tr skipped in last row, rep from *, working last sc in sc at end of row and changing to B with last yo of this last sc. Turn. Drop A at side of work, but do not break off.

6th patt row Using B, ch3, skip first sc, *1dc in next st, 1hdc in next st, ch1, skip next st (tr), 1hdc in next st, 1dc in next st, 1tr in top of tr 2 rows below (in same place as sc in last row), rep from *, working last tr in sc at end of row. Turn.

Rep 3rd–6th patt rows to form diamond patt and cont until 24 rows have been worked from beg (6 rows of B diamonds), ending with a 4th patt row in A. Still using A, work edging as foll:

Edging rnd Using A, ch1, 3sc in first sc, [1sc in each of next 5 sts, 1sc in top of tr skipped in last row] 4 times, 1sc in each of next 5sc, 3sc in last sc; cont along side of piece working 29sc evenly spaced; along foundation-ch edge work 3sc in first ch, 1sc in each ch to last ch, 3sc in last ch; work 29sc evenly along second side; join with a sl st in first sc of rnd. Fasten off.

finishing touches

Weave in any loose ends on the WS.

Border

Place the crochet front on top of back, with WS tog and with sc edgings lined up. Join layers by working dc around outer edge as foll:

Using a 10.00mm (US size N-13) hook and C and working through both layers, join yarn to any corner sc with a sl st, ch3, 2dc in same place as sl st, then work 1dc in each sc around three sides of cushion, working 3dc in each corner sc; along fourth side work 1dc in each sc but through one layer only to make an opening for inserting pillow-form/cushion pad; join with a sl st in 3rd of ch3.

Decorative weaving

Weave C through 2 rows as foll:

Cut three 1yd/91cm strands of C and thread onto a yarn needle. Weave yarns through sts across top row of diamonds in A, and then back across row again. Secure ends at seam.

Weave C through next row of diamonds in A in same way.

Fabric cushion cover

To make fabric cover, pin one back piece to each side of front and sew seams with a 1/2in/1.5cm seam allowance. Turn under and stitch 1/2in/1.5cm hems along outer edges of backs (edges that will be along opening). Then fold backs onto front with RS tog and stitch rem seams, leaving overlapping edges open. Turn RS out and press.

Insert pillow-form/cushion-pad in fabric cover, then put this inside crochet cover. Sew opening closed with invisible stitches.

yarn-and-rag cushion

Mohair yarn and douppioni silk are two of my favorite materials for crochet. When crocheting swatches to test my color scheme, I noticed how attractive the stray strands of fabric and yarn at the edge of the crochet were. Instead of trying to hide these, I decided to make them the star attraction of the design by tying them in knots to form a tasseled edging. Using this simple stitch pattern of alternating chain-spaces and single crochet produces a much softer effect than single crochet does when worked on its own.

here's how...

If preferred, you can make the cushion without the self-fringe. To do this, work the first two rows of the front as for the back, then work in stripes as directed, but changing to the new color with the last loop of the previous row (see page 89).

how big is it?
The finished cushion measures approximately 17in/42.5cm square.

which stitches?
- Single crochet (sc)
- Chain spaces (ch-sp)

how much yarn?
MC = medium-weight mohair yarn in main color
  9 x 1³/₄oz/50g balls Rowan *Kid Classic*
  (light blue—shade no. 818—or chosen color)
A = silk fabric strips in first contrasting color
  ¹/₃yd/30cm of 44in/112cm wide coral douppioni silk
B = medium-weight mohair yarn in second contrasting color
  1 x 1³/₄oz/50g ball Rowan *Kid Classic*
  (pink—shade no. 819—or chosen color)
C = silk fabric strips in third contrasting color
  ¹/₃yd/30cm of 44in/112cm wide mid blue douppioni silk

try this!

If your white pillow-form/cushion pad shows through your crochet, cover it with a cotton fabric that matches the main yarn.

D = medium-weight mohair yarn in fourth contrasting color
  1 x 1³/₄oz/50g ball Rowan *Kid Classic*
  (orange—shade no. 827—or chosen color)
E = silk fabric strips in fifth contrasting color
  ¹/₃yd/30cm of 44in/112cm wide terracotta douppioni silk
(*See page 124 for yarn tips*)

which hook?
12.00mm (US size O/P-15) crochet hook

what gauge?
8¹/₂ sts and 9 rows to 4in/10cm measured over patt st using four strands MC held tog and 12.00mm (US size O/P-15) hook.

any extras?
Pillow-form/cushion pad to fit

before you start
- This pattern is formed with chain-spaces (ch-sp) and single crochet. The chain-space is formed by working a chain and leaving the stitch under it unworked. When working into a "ch-sp," insert the hook through the space under the chain (not into the chain itself).
- Cut (or tear) your silk rag strips ³/₄in/2cm wide (see opposite and page 97).
- *For crochet abbreviations, turn to page 127.*

make the foundation chain
The cushion is made in three pieces—a front with stripes and two plain overlapping back pieces.
Front
Using a 12.00mm (US size O/P-15) hook and four strands MC, ch36 and fasten off, leaving 7in/17.5cm

long loose ends at each end of foundation ch. Using a separate length of each color for each row and leaving 7in/17.5cm loose ends at each end of each row, beg patt as foll:

1st row Using four strands MC, join MC with a sl st to first ch, ch1, 1sc in same place as sl st, *ch1, skip next ch, 1sc in next ch; rep from * to last ch, 1sc in last ch. Turn. (36 sts, counting each sc and each ch1 as one st) Fasten off.

2nd row Using four strands MC, join MC with a sl st to first sc, ch1, 1sc in same place as sl st, *ch1, 1sc in next ch1-sp; rep from * to last sc, 1sc in last sc. Turn. Fasten off.

Rep last row to form patt (fastening off after each row and using four strands of MC, B, and D), **and at the same time** work in stripes as foll:

4 rows more MC, **1 row A, 1 row B, 1 row C, 1 row D, 1 row E, and 6 rows MC.**

Rep from ** to ** twice more. Fasten off.

Backs (make 2 alike)

Using a 12.00mm (US size O/P-15) hook and four strands MC, ch37.

1st row 1sc in 2nd ch from hook, *ch1, skip next ch, 1sc in next ch; rep from * to last ch, 1sc in last ch. Turn. (36 sts, counting each sc and each ch1 as one st)

2nd row Ch1, 1sc in first sc, *ch1, 1sc in next ch1-sp; rep from * to last sc, 1sc in last sc. Turn.

Rep last row to form patt, working until back measures 10³⁄₄in/27cm from foundation-ch edge (approximately 24 rows).

Work last row as foll:

Last row Ch1, 1sc in each of first 2sc, *1sc in next ch1-sp, 1sc in next sc; rep from * to end. Fasten off.

finishing touches

Knot loose ends on front tog in groups to form groups of fringe along sides as foll:

make your own yarn!

If your fabric tears easily, the quickest way to prepare the crochet strips is to tear them. When crocheted up, they look just as good as cut strips. To make a continuous strip of "rag" yarn, first straighten the end of your length of fabric. Then start at the selvage and tear or cut a strip to the required width, stopping near the selvage. It is generally best to stop at a distance from the edge of the fabric that is at least half the width of the strip. Turn and tear or cut in the opposite direction, stopping near the edge as before. Tear or cut back and forth in this way.

First knot ends in MC tog at each end of each MC stripe, positioning knot close to crochet. Then knot ends in A, B, C, D, and E tog at each end of rem stripes (see pages 114–115).

Lay front RS up on a flat surface and fold fringe groups onto RS. Then lay backs on top of front with RS facing, overlapping them at center to form an envelope opening. Pin in place. Using two strands MC, overcast stitch backs to front all around outside edge (see page 120 for how to work overcast stitch). Turn RS and trim fringe groups 2³⁄₄in/7cm from each knot. Insert pillow-form/cushion pad.

useful things to know

seams and linings...

seams for huge-hook crochet

For a good finish, stitching seams on huge-hook crochet needs to be done quite carefully. Any flaws in seams are more obvious than on smaller-scale crocheted textures. The best method to use is a simple overcast stitch. For seams that show on the outside, double-sided backstitch makes a neat finishing touch. A cushion made from two circular pieces would be a good candidate for a decorative outside seam (see the tip box on page 98). Pieces of "rag" crochet should be stitched together either with a shallow overcast stitch, or edge-to-edge with a slip stitch, using a sewing needle and a strong sewing thread.

To weave in loose ends on huge-hook crochet, use a blunt-ended needle or a fine crochet hook to weave invisibly into the stitches. Split really thick yarns into two strands and weave in each strand separately. Clip off the woven-in ends close to the crochet. If the crochet has a wrong side that will not show, such as inside a cushion cover, you can knot together the loose ends, instead of weaving them in, and clip off close to the knot.

Working an overcast seam

Work the overcast stitches close to the edge of the two pieces of crochet. Use a blunt-ended yarn needle and matching yarn if the piece has been crocheted with yarn, and a sewing needle and thread if it has been worked with fabric strips. Place the two pieces with right sides together and edges aligned. Pin if necessary. Take a couple of stitches in the same place to start, then work stitches at equal intervals, as shown top right. Secure with a couple of stitches.

Working a double-sided backstitch seam

The double-sided backstitch looks like backstitch on both the front and the back of the work, so it is perfect for decorative, outside seams. Every other stitch on each side of the seam is double, but this will not be obvious on the finished seam since the second stitch completely covers the first stitch, matching it exactly.

Make the first stitch on the underside and work a stitch backward on the other side of the crochet to match it, then make a stitch over the first stitch as shown by the arrow (A). Continue working the stitches as shown below, following the illustrations (B and C). Repeat steps A, B, and C along the seam (working two stitches forward, then one stitch backward).

OVERCAST SEAM

DOUBLE-SIDED BACKSTITCH

A B C

linings for huge-hook crochet

Bags and totes that get a lot of use are best strengthened with a fabric lining. Cushion covers crocheted with huge hooks are also best lined, since the white pillow-form/cushion pad inside can show through the large textures. These linings are simply slipped on over the bare pillow-form/cushion pad before the crochet cover is put on.

If the lining fabric shows through the crochet, make sure that the color of the lining matches the main yarn used. If the lining won't show through—for instance, inside a closely crocheted bag or tote—you can choose a complementary color or print.

FLAT BAG LINING

A   B

SHAPED BAG LINING

A   B

Lining a simple flat bag

A bag made of two squares or rectangles is really easy to line (see Single-crochet Bags on page 60). Use the crocheted front of your bag to calculate the size of the two bag lining pieces. Add extra to the base and both sides for the 1/2 in/1.5cm seam allowances and about 1 1/2 in/4cm at the top for a hem.

Cut two pieces of fabric to the correct size and place them with right sides together. Stitch 1/2 in/ 1.5cm from the edge around the two sides and bottom, leaving the top open (A). Press the top of the side seams open, then fold down the top hem and press (B). Insert the lining in the bag and stitch it invisibly to the bag along the hem fold.

Lining a shaped bag

Lining a three-dimensional bag, such as the Bag with Rag Strap on page 72, is a little more difficult, but the principle is the same. Use the finished bag as the guide for cutting the lining. Measure the bag from the top edge, around the bottom, and to the top on the other side. Then measure it around the width of the bag. Allowing for 1/2 in/1.5cm seam allowances at the sides and for 1 1/2 in/4cm hems at the top, cut the lining as one piece. If desired you can press an iron-on interfacing onto the fabric pieces before stitching them together to give the lining body.

Fold the lining in half widthwise, stitch the side seams, turn down the top hem, clip off the corners at the bottom (A). Then press the seams open, pinch together a triangle shape at the two bottom corners and stitch across them as shown (B). Fold the triangle points to the underside of the bag shape as shown by the arrows to make a simple box shape. Insert the prepared lining into the bag and stitch to the inside of the bag along the hem fold.

trims for huge-hook crochet...

decorative finishes

Huge-hook crochet looks great with added decorative trims, handmade or readymade. There are countless pretty finishing touches available these days—tassels, fringe, ribbons, pompoms, braids, beads, and sequins. All you need to do is stitch them to your finished crocheted project. You might even want to design the crochet to suit the trim, rather than the other way around. It's a good way to use up delectable trims that you have collected, but don't know what to do with.

The pompoms, beads, tassels, and fringes I've used on my designs are just examples of how you can decorate and personalize your own crochet. Making your own trims is more satisfying than buying them. If you're new to crochet, you may not know how to make the three simple popular trims that avid crocheters often use—pompoms (instructions for how to make pompoms are given on page 53), tassels, and fringes. You can make fringes and tassels from any yarn you like, a mixture of yarns, or even ribbon, strung beads, or fabric strips.

Although your huge-hook crochet is done in a flash, take your time with handmade trims. Never rush finishing touches. Perfect, carefully finished trims will add that extra professional touch that makes your crochet a real eyecatcher.

Making a tassel

To make a tassel, first cut lots of strands of yarn, a little longer than twice the desired length of the tassel. Hold the strands together and tie a separate length of yarn tightly around the center (A). (Leave the ends of the tying yarn long to use for fastening to your crochet.) Fold the tassel strands in half at the tie and wrap another length of yarn around them to form a "ball" of strands at the top and secure (B).

Making a fringe

To make a fringe, first cut a length of yarn at least 1in/2.5cm longer than the desired length of the finished fringe and fold it in half. (For a plumper fringe, use two or more strands together.) Insert a crochet hook from back to front through the edge of the crochet and draw the yarn through. Then draw the ends of the yarn through the loop (A) and pull to tighten. Work the fringe as close together or far apart as desired (B). When the fringe is complete, trim the ends to even them.

MAKING A TASSEL

A   B

MAKING A FRINGE

A   B

MAKING A TWISTED CORD

A

B

C

decorative fastenings and straps

The fastenings you use on bags and cushions, and the straps and handles for bags, are important finishing touches that can turn them into something really special. When creating your own huge-hook projects, focus a lot of attention on the style of the items you pick for these. Fastenings for bags can be buttons, buckles, or drawstrings; for cushions: buttons and cord ties. Avoid zippers to keep the techniques as simple as possible.

As for the straps and handles on my bag designs, there are wooden handles, crocheted leather and yarn ones, and twisted cords. Hopefully, you'll think of even more decorative fastenings, straps, and handles for your own designs. Search craft stores and fabric stores for enticing readymade cords, ribbons, and braids.

Ever wondered how you could use those delectable, unique huge buttons found in flea markets? They are ideal for huge-hook handbags and totes, and cushions. Often on huge-hook textures there's no need for buttonholes either—the buttons will pass right through the crochet.

Twisted cords feature a lot in my designs, so there are instructions for how to make them yourself on this page. A single yarn or a mixture of yarns can be used to make them. Or you can introduce a fabric strip or thin ribbon for an unusual effect. For clarity, only a single strand is shown in the instructions, but for thick cords you will need to start out with at least

two strands. There is no hard and fast rule about how long to cut the strands for a specific length of twisted cord, as it depends on how stretchy the yarn is and on how tightly the cord is twisted. You will, however, need strands that are at least twice the length of the finished cord since they are folded in half to form the twist. For the twisted cords used for the projects in this book, I have indicated how many strands of yarn to use and how long to cut them.

Making a twisted cord

Cut the number of strands required, to the length specified. Then tie one end of the group of strands to a fixed object—I use a door handle. Tie the other end to a pencil. Hold the yarn loosely in one hand at the pencil end and with the other hand turn the pencil round and round (A). Keep the yarn taut as you twist it. Once the yarn starts to kink, fold it in half, still keeping it taut. Let one half of the yarn twist around the other half, releasing it gradually (B). Cut the ends of the yarn from the door handle and pencil and knot them together. Tie a knot at the folded end as well and trim off the ends (C).

buying yarn...

Yarn manufacturers change their yarn colors quite often, so it is almost impossible to guarantee that all the shades in the book will still be available when you use this book. The shade numbers used are given in the instructions if you want to use them, but feel free to use your own choice of colors.

When possible, try to buy the specific brand and type of yarn recommended in the pattern (see page 126 for addresses). However, if you need to use a substitute, be sure to buy yarn by figuring out how many yards/meters you need rather than how much in weight.

The Rowan and Colinette yarns used in this book are listed here to help you find a comparable substitute. The life-size photos of the yarns will help you find a yarn of a similar thickness. The knitting gauge and needle size given for each yarn can also be used to identify yarn thickness.

Rowan yarns used in this book

All Seasons Cotton
- A medium-weight cotton yarn; 60% cotton and 40% acrylic/microfiber
- 1³⁄₄oz/50g (approximately 98yd/90m) per ball
- Recommended gauge: 16–18 sts and 23–25 rows to 4in/10cm over St st using 4¹⁄₂–5¹⁄₂mm (US size 7–9) knitting needles

Biggy Print
- A superchunky wool yarn; 100% merino wool
- 3¹⁄₂oz/100g (approximately 33yd/30m) per ball
- Recommended gauge: 5¹⁄₂ sts and 7 rows to 4in/10cm over St st using 20mm (US size 35) knitting needles

Big Wool
- A superchunky wool yarn; 100% merino wool
- 3¹⁄₂oz/100g (approximately 87yd/80m) per ball
- Recommended gauge: 7¹⁄₂–8 sts and 10–12 rows to 4in/10cm over St st using 12mm or 15mm (US size 17 or 19) knitting needles

Chunky Cotton Chenille
- A chunky cotton chenille yarn; 100% cotton
- 3¹⁄₂oz/100g (approximately 153yd/140m) per ball
- Recommended gauge: 16–18 sts and 21–25 rows to 4in/10cm over St st using 4¹⁄₂–5mm (US size 7–8) knitting needles

Cotton Tape
- A tubular tape yarn; 100% cotton
- 1³⁄₄oz/50g (approximately 71yd/65m) per ball
- Recommended gauge: 13–14 sts and 17–19 rows to 4in/10cm over St st using 8mm (US size 11) knitting needles

Kid Classic
- A medium-weight mohair yarn; 70% lambswool, 26% kid mohair, and 4% nylon
- 1³⁄₄oz/50g (approximately 153yd/140m) per ball
- Recommended gauge: 18–19 sts and 23–25 rows to 4in/10cm over St st using 5–5¹⁄₂mm (US size 8–9) knitting needles

Kid Silk Haze
- A fine mohair yarn; 70% super kid mohair and 30% silk
- 1oz/25g (approximately 229yd/210m) per ball
- Recommended gauge: 18–25 sts and 23–34 rows to 4in/10cm over St st using 3¹⁄₄–5mm (US size 3–8) knitting needles

Linen Print

- A tubular tape yarn; 70% viscose and 30% linen
- 1³/₄oz/50g (approximately 60yd/55m) per ball
- Recommended gauge: 13 sts and 16 rows to 4in/10cm over St st using 8mm (US size 11) knitting needles

Polar

- A chunky wool yarn; 60% pure new wool, 30% alpaca, and 10% acrylic
- 3¹/₂oz/100g (approximately 109yd/100m) per ball
- Recommended gauge: 12 sts and 16 rows to 4in/10cm over St st using 8mm (US size 11) knitting needles

Summer Tweed

- A lightweight silk and cotton blend yarn; 70% silk and 30% cotton
- 1³/₄oz/50g (approximately 118yd/108m) per hank
- Recommended gauge: 16 sts and 23 rows to 4in/10cm over St st using 5mm (US size 8) knitting needles

Colinette yarns used in this book

Point 5

- A chunky yarn; 100% pure wool
- 3¹/₂oz/100g (approximately 54yd/50m) per hank
- Recommended gauge: 7¹/₂ sts and 9 rows to 4in/10cm over St st using 12mm (US size 17) knitting needles

Rowan *All Seasons Cotton*

Rowan *Biggy Print*

Rowan *Big Wool*

Rowan *Chunky Cotton Chenille*

Rowan *Cotton Tape*

Rowan *Kid Classic*

Rowan *Kid Silk Haze*

Rowan *Linen Print*

Rowan *Polar*

Rowan *Summer Tweed*

Colinette *Point 5*

addresses...

addresses for buying yarns

To find out where to buy Rowan or Colinette yarns near you, contact their websites:
www.knitrowan.com
www.colinette.com

For the Lion Brand novelty tape yarn shown on page 14, contact the Lion Brand website listed under Addresses for Huge Hooks (see right).

for quilting or fabric knitting supplies

Cotton Patch Mail Order
3404 Hall Lane
Dept. CTB
Lafayette, CA 94549
800-835-4418
925-283-7883
email: quiltusa@yahoo.com
website: www.quiltusa.com

Note: Fabric and yarn used in the items featured may not currently be available because manufacturers keep most products in print for only a short time.

addresses for huge hooks

Try Lion Brand if, like me, you can't bear using drab gray hooks—they have a nice range of big hooks in bright colors. Alternatively, contact Needles! (in North Carolina), where you'll find a massive range of interesting hooks.

Lion Brand website: www.lionbrandyarn.com
Needles! website: jklneedles.com

for more information

Ask for a free catalog:
C&T Publishing, Inc.
P.O. Box 1456
Lafayette, CA 94549
800-284-1114
email: ctinfo@ctpub.com
website: www.ctpub.com

author's acknowledgments...

First of all, I'd like to thank the team who put this book together. Thanks to John Heseltine for his stunning photographs, to Anne Wilson for her wonderful book design, and to Kate Simunek for all the fantastic illustrations. Many thanks also to Anna Sanderson and Auberon Hedgecoe at Mitchell Beazley for making this project possible and helping it to run so smoothly, and to Kate Buller and Ann Hinchcliffe at Rowan for getting me the Rowan yarns I needed so swiftly.

Thanks to my friend Nancy Thomas at Lion Brand Yarns for supplying me with colored crochet hooks at a moment's notice and for loving knitting and crochet as much as I do.

My gratitude goes most of all to Susan Berry for her expertise on every aspect of the book process, including art direction of my crochet design, and for making me believe I could author this book.

crochet abbreviations...

To make crochet instructions easier to follow, they are written with the use of abbreviations. The abbreviations used are very logical and quick to learn, and the ones used in this book are as follows:

alt	alternate
beg	begin(ning)
ch	chain(s)
ch-sp	chain space
CC	contrasting color
cm	centimeter(s)
cont	continu(e)(ing)
dc	double crochet
dec	decreas(e)(ing)
dtr	double treble
foll	follow(s)(ing)
g	gram(s)
hdc	half double crochet
inc	increas(e)(ing)
lp(s)	loop(s)
m	meter(s)
MC	main color
mm	millimeter(s)
oz	ounces
patt	pattern
rem	remain(s)(ing)
rep	repeat(s)(ing)
rnd(s)	round(s)
RS	right side
sc	single crochet
sl st	slip stitch
sp	space(s)
st(s)	stitch(es)
tog	together
tr	treble crochet
trtr	triple treble
WS	wrong side
yd	yard(s)
yo	yarn over hook

* Repeat instructions after asterisk or between asterisks as many times as instructed.

[ ] ( ) Repeat instructions inside square brackets or parentheses as many times as instructed.

English-language terminology

The names for the basic crochet stitches are different in the US and UK, which can be confusing if you pick up a crochet book when abroad. This book is written with US crochet terminology throughout. If you are a British crocheter, be sure to follow the patterns with the following in mind!

US	UK
slip stitch (sl st)	slip stitch (ss)
single crochet (sc)	double crochet (dc)
half double crochet (hdc)	half treble crochet (htr)
double crochet (dc)	treble crochet (tr)
treble crochet (tr)	double treble (dtr)
double treble (dtr)	triple treble (trtr)
triple treble (trtr)	quadruple treble (qtr)
quadruple treble (qtr)	quintuple treble (quintr)
yarn over hook (yo)	yarn round hook (yrh)
skip (stitches)	miss (stitches)

crochet hook conversion chart

This chart shows you how the different crochet hook size systems compare, though the numbering and lettering sizes can vary from manufacturer to manufacturer. Since metric sizes are based on the diameter of the hook and tend to be more exact than the numbering or lettering size, it is best to follow these.

US sizes	EU Metric	US sizes	EU Metric
14 steel	.60mm	G-6	4.00mm
12 steel	.75mm	7	4.50mm
11 steel	1.00mm	H-8	5.00mm
7 steel	1.25mm	I-9	5.50mm
6 steel	1.50mm	J-10	6.00mm
5 steel	1.75mm	K-10$\frac{1}{2}$	6.50mm
	2.00mm		7.00mm
B-1 (2.25mm)		L-11	8.00mm
	2.50mm	M	9.00mm
C-2 (2.75mm)		N-13	10.00mm
	3.00mm	O/P-15	12.00mm
D-3 (3.25mm)		Q	15.00mm
E-4	3.50mm	S	20.00mm
F-5 (3.75mm)			

index...